Trends in International Taxation

David W. Williams
Price Waterhouse Professor of International Business Taxation,
University of London

International Fiscal Association
British Branch

IBFD Publications bv
P.O. Box 20237
1000 HE Amsterdam
Telephone: +31 (0)20 - 626-7726

ISBN 90.70125-53.6
NUGI 696

Preface

The aim of this essay is to explore the international effects of national tax changes, and the effects of changes in one national tax system on other tax systems. Its subject matter is, for many people, one of the most arcane and abstruse areas of human endeavour. Perhaps that is why so many tolerate its effects in ignorance of its workings. The irony is that it is an area of activity which can have just about as much effect on the general human endeavour as any other.

That is a bold statement, but its justification is simple. By definition taxes are those funds payable by compulsion to government. Any society which purports to exercise any level of activity whatsoever other than purely voluntary activity or the activity of forced labour, or any society which seeks to transfer or redistribute funds in any way within itself, will resort to taxing techniques to do so. It is a requirement as basic as the wheel is to transport, or electricity is to computers.

Because tax is so important as a technique of government, its influence on behaviour is potentially so far reaching. Yet most of those who seek to impose taxes, and most of those who choose the legislators, know – and, it would seem, wish to know – nothing about the mysteries of raising taxes, at least for most of the time. This essay discusses the effects of a period when that is a little less true – when 'reform' is the order of the day.

This is not a textbook or a commentary on tax laws, nor yet a history, nor is it intended to be. That is why little attempt has been made to provide references to, and criticism of, sources with the academic rigour that such works would rightly require. Even so, because of the subject matter, this is an attempt at the impossible. It is a personal note of reflection upon what has been happening to tax systems, and what might be happening to them. Whilst it has been based upon both wide readings and wide discussion, it is bound both to be wrong in parts, and out of date in parts, as to its facts – as would any other similar volume. It may also be wrong in its ideas. Only time will reveal how far wrong. The essay is offered in the conviction that its subject is too important to be left just to time, whilst too abstruse to catch the attention of many.

Insofar as this essay is right in fact or law, my thanks are due to a great many people. I have had the tremendous advantage of the comments both of my colleagues and my students on the International Tax Course in London over the last three years. Nothing is more salutory to the teacher than to be caught pontificating on something by a student who says simply 'It doesn't happen that way in Peru' – or France, or Panama, or Malta, or Hong Kong, or Switzerland, or South Africa, or Greece, or Denmark, or Israel, or Singapore, or the UK, or Poland, or Australia, or Norway, or the USA, or Spain, or India, or Czechoslovakia, or the Netherlands, or China, or Belgium, or Japan, or Italy, or Colombia, or Germany, or Zimbabwe, or Canada, or Ethiopia, or Trinidad, or Hungary, or . . . Grateful thanks to them all, and in particular to Philip Baker, Kees Van Raad, John Avery

Jones and the others who have taught on that course.

A list of these and others whom I must thank because I have been privileged to speak with them in the last three years would be presumptuous. Suffice to say that I have had the enormous privilege of conferences, lectures and conversations in, or with those from, a range of countries that leaves little of the atlas untouched.

From them all, I must confine myself to three offers of thanks. First, to Arfan Sheikh, my research assistant during the first year of this study, and whose industrious beavering led to the collation of details of tax systems from around the world, and also to Sandra Baird my secretary. Next, to the British Branch of the IFA for generously granting me the funds to employ Arfan and undertake this work, and especially the committee of its trustees (consisting of John Avery Jones, David Davidson, Brian Houghton, John Hickman and John Phillips) whose joint and several comments on this study, based on a combined wealth of insight and experience that would be difficult to rival, did much to guide and counsel. They must also be thanked for encouraging and facilitating the publication of this work. Finally, to Price Waterhouse for the simple but most generous fact that they made it possible for my job to exist.

This essay attempts to reflect on tax affairs up to the end of 1990. It tries not to do so just from the perspective of the western end of Europe, but inevitably my own background in the UK shapes my thoughts. My apologies for that and all else which is wrong when so many have tried to make it right.

David W Williams
University of London
January 1991.

Contents

Chapter 1

Introduction

> For good ye are and bad, and like to coins,
> Some true, some light, but every one of you
> Stamp'd with the image of the King.
> Tennyson, The Holy Grail.

100. When countries from Algeria to Zimbabwe in the space of a few years, and not under the pressures of war, find it necessary to talk of the need to change their tax systems, it is also necessary for observers to question and ponder. Not least must they ponder why it is that politicians consider it worth their while to talk about taxation at all. The whole of recorded history evidences the political opprobrium to be earned by the imposition of unpopular taxes and adds to it the rider that, bar exceptional circumstances, taxes are, almost by definition, unpopular. For this simple reason, the cliche that 'an old tax is a good tax' suggests that a new tax is the converse.

101. Despite this accepted wisdom, we read regularly of more tax reforms in more states. Something, somewhere, must have gone wrong for politicians to find it necessary to introduce changes into a system their instincts tell them to leave alone.

102. That it has been felt, in many states, that all was not well with their tax systems has now been evidenced very widely. As wc argue in this essay, this is undoubtedly an age of tax reform or at least of tax change of a kind one does not usually see. That invites comments from many : the historian, the political scientist, the administrator, the economist, the legislator, the politician and, of course, the practitioner of accounting, law and tax. So far there has been much comment by some of these categories: the economist and the political scientist above all. Other areas have invited less attention, one being the effect of reforms on international taxation. That is the topic examined in this essay.

103. To set the scene for this essay, this chapter addresses definitions and points of methodology necessary to our approach, and indicates the directions of the work.

International taxation

104. The regularly repeated truism that 'there is no such thing as international taxation – show me an international tax demand' is, perhaps, the best starting point. The first concern is to the terms used, and the first of those is taxation. This discussion adopts the OECD working definition (see the annual volumes of Revenue Statistics) that the term 'taxes' is confined to compulsory, unrequited payments to general government. It clearly excludes any charges or penalties, but includes any specific taxes, such as social security payments made by compulsion. The reason for adopting this wide definition is to emphasise the scope of this study. 'Tax reform' is sometimes couched in individual countries in deliberately narrow terms. For many, social security contributions are 'not tax'. Neither are annual company registration charges imposed instead of a corporate profits tax. A different line is often drawn between 'tax' and 'customs duties', particularly anti-dumping duties, with some countries regarding border taxes as part of trade relations rather than taxation. For the purposes of this study, all those categories are included as tax, as are any transfer payments within government to the central funds of the state from, for example, a trading arm of government – even though, again, some would reject this as not being part of 'tax'.

105. The common element is that the payment is made without any option on the part of the payor, and without direct consideration on the part of the state. Within that definition, it is increasingly important to appreciate all the different kinds of taxes, and the parts they play in a state's overall taxing operation. This is because one undoubted shift in recent years has been into wider forms of revenue.

106. One area of 'tax' in its widest sense is excluded from the study. This is the area of negative taxes or subsidies, except where they take the form of tax expenditures, that is, exceptions, exemptions, reliefs or failures to tax which are part of the taxing system. A grant by central government to support the building of a factory in a depressed area is not 'tax' in the sense used here if it is not a part of the tax system (for example, by allowing the cost to be written off). It must be noted, having said that, that another aspect of changes in public finances in recent years has been the shift away from such subsidies both within and without the tax system of a state.

107. Against this definition of tax, 'international tax' does not make logical or semantic sense, unless we find (as we do with the European Communities) supranational taxing powers. Rather, our concern here is with the cross-frontier or trans-national aspects of national taxes and tax systems, that is, the interactions that arise because states tax persons or

transactions in circumstances when other states also tax those persons or transactions. We are concerned, in this sense, with conflicts of laws and jurisdictions and the effects and resolutions of those conflicts. We are also concerned with the rules of public law within which such effects and resolutions occur.

108. International tax is of concern largely because it gives rise to distortions of national systems either by imposing higher levels of taxation on a taxpayer than would have occurred under one system operating alone, or because it allows a taxpayer to pay a lower level of tax than would have occurred internally to a state. States also have a third concern, though it is not so obviously the concern of the taxpayer. They are directly interested in whether they get 'their' share of the total taxes paid by the taxpayer, as compared with any other state involved.

109. International taxation, then, is concerned with two issues relating to the imposition of national taxes. First is the extent to which the interaction of national tax systems cause a change in the total level of taxes payable by taxpayers. Second is the extent to which the interaction causes the tax revenues to be collected by one national authority rather than another.

Tax reform

110. The theme explored in this essay is the changes that are or may be occurring to international taxation caused by the tax reform noted above. What is a 'tax reform'? That is a very difficult term to define because the assessment of whether something should be termed a 'reform' is highly political in itself. It is expedient, in some contexts, to dress up as 'reform' a mere transient trimming of a system, whilst in other contexts it is better to disguise the extent of change, or to present part of a change whilst disguising some other part. The political sensitivity of imposed payments means that such presentational issues are of major importance in the present context.

111. Because of this deliberate obfuscation, no definition is attempted that is related to what has been regarded as reform domestically. Rather, changes are noted in a system which will have, or which appear to be intended to have, more than a short-term effect. Mere changes of rates at the margin are not reforms, nor are the adding or subtracting of particular allowances. The reform, if there is one, lies under these particulars in changing attitudes rather than details. Rate changes which are intended to mark a different attitude to a tax are clearly of significance, as is a determined attitude either to increasing or decreasing the use of allowances.

112. According to some, new taxes should be a major sign of reform, although the purist has rightly pointed out that 'an innovation is not a 're-form"(Burke). As noted below, there are those who have looked in vain for these new taxes and have found but little (the British Community Charge apart). Several such new taxes have been proposed : the expenditure tax has perhaps the longest pedigree, but there is also the cash-flow corporation tax, and the wider use of taxes such as the net wealth tax.

113. It is not of concern to examine here whether these alternatives *should* be adopted as reforms, nor to criticise from a policy aspect those reforms which have been adopted. That is for the politician, the political scientist or the economist, and all have already been busy on this theme. An attempt is made to resist the temptation to add new ideas of my own, and I apologise where the text has lapsed from that objective, for it is a distraction. Rather, the concern is with the reforms that *have* happened, or are said to be happening, and their consequences and effects.

Scope of this study

114. In summary, this study concentrates on the extent to which reform is actually taking place in national tax systems, and the effect of such reforms on international taxation, that is, on the total taxes payable by any taxpayer, and on the sharing between states of tax revenues from any one taxpayer. It is concerned with the effect on international taxation of the trends of national tax reforms. The task is to survey what has happened to reform systems (if anything), to identify within the individual states' actions any trends or patterns of change, and to examine the effects that those trends or patterns might have on international taxation.

115. The study is tackled in two stages. First, we examine what has been happening in a number of states so as to identify any trends. We then examine and explore the trends and patterns, so as to indicate issues requiring to be examined at international level. In the second part of the study, we take these trends and patterns and attempt to test them against the problems of international taxation and, in particular, the mechanisms used to deal with international taxation. Above all, that means that our attention was directed to double taxation relief and the mechanisms available to deal with it.

116. The thrust of this study is qualitative rather than quantitative. By that is meant that an attempt is made by argument and example to explore the issues raised and to advance conclusions and issues requiring resolution. There is no attempt exhaustively to describe, or to produce figures.

Partly, this is because others have already done this. Our concern is with an area that has received less attention, and we can start on the solid basis of work already published.

The work already done

117. A full list of alterations could be achieved by a detailed compilation through or from such works as the two annual volumes produced by Price Waterhouse, *Corporate Taxes – A Worldwide Summary* and *Individual Taxes – A Worldwide Summary*, and equivalent volumes produced by others, including Coopers and Lybrand, Deloittes and Touche Ross, or the more detailed studies by the International Bureau of Fiscal Documentation, supported by the surveys in *Tax News Service*. Reliance is placed on all these sources in this essay.

Likewise, there are figures available in the annual relevant reports of national and international bodies, of which the annual *OECD Revenue Statistics*, the annual *IMF* reports, and the annual *World Development Report* of the World Bank are particularly valuable, and are relied on in this essay. However, as noted below, those figures deal only with part of the problem. They give valuable data to allow national comparisons, but little to study international interactions.

118. Most of the profiles in such works are individual or comparative national studies. This is of course true of most national studies. Insofar as they are concerned (as those of, say, the Netherlands, Australia and Canada have been concerned) with international issues, it is chiefly with the competitive position of the national tax systems as related to others. It is also true, though to a lesser extent, of the comments and studies of the international bodies. The work of the World Bank, reflected particularly in the 1988 *World Development Report,* is aimed at the improvement of the public finances of its client states, and therefore to aspects of international taxation. It has been and is actively involved in assisting, advising and monitoring tax policy and administration.

119. *The International Monetary Fund*'s work is aimed wider, and has given rise to two recent invaluable studies, that by Tait on *Value Added Tax*, and that by Newbury and others on the *Theory of Taxation in Developing States*. Both have been influential in the reform process itself. The IMF advisers have also been active in their advice to developing states and, in particular, the new democracies of central and eastern Europe, giving the IMF a direct opportunity to put its ideas into practice in individual states.

120. More important, from the standpoint of the fully developed states, is the on-going work of the Fiscal Affairs Committee of the OECD. This has produced a steady series of reports of major importance in the last few years, all of which have been of great value to us in working on this study. In particular, the 1986 report on *Personal Income Tax Systems under Changing Economic Conditions*, when read with the reports and papers in the 1987 *Taxation in Developed Countries* gives a strong base for any discussion of reform. This is then supplemented by a number of reports on more detailed areas of relevance, *Tax Expenditures* (1984), *Taxation of Net Wealth, Capital Transfers and Capital Gains of Individuals* (1988), *Taxation of Fringe Benefits* (1989), *Taxing Consumption* (1989), and the various volumes on specific international taxation issues.

121. Besides these major contributions, there have been a number of private discussions and seminars. Probably the most influential was the seminar held in 1987 by the Brookings Institution of the USA which reviewed developments in eleven major states, and invited the comments of some of th world's leading tax economists upon them. Its papers were published as *World Tax Reform: A Progress Report.* At about the same time some of those contributors, along with others, gave papers to a published Symposium on Tax Reform, published in Economic Perspectives in the summer of 1987. Third, the University of Virginia took a different approach in a subsequent seminar in looking ahead to the shape of the tax system in the twenty-first century, some papers for which were published in 1988.

122. To this list must be added many more smaller and individual contributions, reflected in the selected bibliography to this study. The result is a mammoth pile of books, articles, and press cuttings, let alone official reports, new statutes and other official publications. This presented a challenge in its own right. A study like this is a snapshot. It can never be up to date. There is therefore limited value in detailing particular systems at a practitioner level. In preparing this text, several dozen position papers were drawn up concerning different states and the reforms that had occurred there. These are not included in this volume. In addition, some details will date fast, from the very nature of our subject. For these reasons, the temptation to annotate and footnote is resisted in the belief that these would distract more than they would aid.

An interim report?

123. A major premiss of all three of the major international symposia is that this is unfinished business. The concern was to look to what had been achieved, either to justify it or to examine how far there were reforms to

be carried out. It is clear from both these sources and what is happening around the world in individual states that reform is unfinished business.

124. To answer the questions raised by current reforms therefore involves gazing into crystal balls – which, as one senior Revenue officer observed at a conference on tax reforms recently, are just one kind of balls. There are major aspects of this subject which are not ball-gazing, however, and which increasingly preoccupy current political debate – issues such as the greying population and other demographic trends which, devastation apart, will alter our tax systems like so much else.

125. Perhaps for the first time in our history, we can now look ahead to some extent and make a few intelligent and informed guesses about what is to be, because we have, through information technology, the capacity to know so much better where we now are and where we have been than used to be the case. The recent OECD reports on Economic Trends do this in the medium term. And administrators and politicians appear, in some states at least, to be anticipating as well as reacting. Very tentatively, I try to do this in this essay.

126. This is therefore another interim report, and it is shaped as such, in that it seeks to draw attention to some of the issues which require more thought, and to some of the questions requiring answers.

Why reform?

127. Before passing on to the descriptive part of this essay, it is worth rehearsing some of the points made in the many national discussions about the reform process. There have been many attempts to formulate reasons for the world-wide interest in reform but not, to borrow Burke's phrase again, innovation. Many draw our attention again to the reasons for taxing, and the factors that make a 'good' tax.

128. At the most generalised level, the need for reform is because it is felt widely that the tax systems we have do not measure very well against the tax systems we should have. Whilst that is a truism, it includes the fundamental point that the process of reform suggests the correction of a system towards the objectives it is currently perceived that it should be serving, rather than the trimming of rates or taxing provisions to deal with particular difficulties or demands. But in measuring reform, we are therefore dealing in large part with political or economic ideals, and these change.

129. It is therefore relevant to ask : have the ideals or objectives of tax systems changed? Are reforms designed to re-establish the status quo

ante – to correct systems that have gone off the rails – or are the systems being changed to align them to new objectives ? That question must be asked both at the national and trans-national level : have individual states changed or reinforced their objectives, and are those changes or reinforcements consistent or divergent as between different countries?

130. One recent United Kingdom review suggests that, at least for the UK, little had changed. In the Green Paper, *Corporation Tax*, (1982), the chapter on "Criteria for Change" started:

> "On the assumption that there will continue to be a corporation tax in one form or another, it is necessary to review briefly the criteria against which the possibility of change needs to be considered. To a significant extent, many of these can still be traced back to the four maxims which Adam Smith formulated in "The Wealth of Nations",
>
> 1. "The subjects of every state ought to contribute towards the support of the government, as nearly as possible, in proportion to their respective abilities; that is, in proportion to the revenue which they respectively enjoy under the protection of the state."
> 2. "The tax which each individual is bound to pay ought to be certain, and not arbitrary."
> 3. "Every tax ought to be levied at the time, or in the manner, it is most likely to be convenient for the contributor to pay it."
> 4. "Every tax ought to be so contrived as both to take out and to keep out of the pockets of the people as little as possible over and above what it brings into the public treasury of the state."
>
> (*The Wealth of Nations*, Book Five, Chapter Two, Part Two.)

It went on to review the criteria under the heads of Equity, Certainty, Simplicity and Cost of Collection, and Economic Criteria, but it significantly added a new criterion, that of international considerations, as to which it said :

> 'The international aspects of business taxation are becoming increasingly important in their own right. It is not simply that many businesses are now organised and operate on an international basis: but also that many businesses which are regarded as – and indeed are – primarily domestic do have important overseas operations. The UK system of company taxation must be capable of application to multinational concerns, overseas shareholders and so on. It must also command a degree of acceptance from the interna-

tional community if difficulties are not to arise in dealings with overseas governments,in particular in achieving proper treatment of the tax in double taxation agreements and in other countries' unilateral provisions for double taxation relief. Any major change in the level or incidence of tax on company profits would affect the balance of advantage between the United Kingdom and other countries. Even if satisfactory agreements could ultimately be reached, there could be serious problems in the meantime in operating under existing agreements with a very substantially changed tax system.'

131. One independent observer regarded this summary as superficial, noting the solemnity and depth of other states' reviews: 'the one document [ie the Green Paper] is essentially trivial relative to the others. Perhaps this comparison is unfair – after all, most things are done better in the United States. But we should be more unhappy about a situation in which material produced by the British government compares so unfavourably with work done in Canada, Australia or New Zealand.' (Kay, 1986).

132. Nonetheless, this echo of traditional objectives is a common theme. It may be doubted whether the Japanese Taxation Commission referred much to Adam Smith, but its report in 1986 was based, according to Aoki (1986) as follows: 'The review was based on the principles of equity, fairness, simplicity, choice and economic vitality taking into consideration the neutrality to resource allocation and the international context.' But so, one might comment, would just about any developed tax system. Is there any consensus on *how* they are to be taken into account?

133. The British objectives have also been restated in Budget Speeches. In 1982, Geoffrey Howe as Chancellor of the Exchequer summarised them as: 'cutting the burden of tax, encouraging wealth creation, and simplifying administration.' They were spelt out, and filled out, more fully in 1985 by his successor, Nigel Lawson:

> 'First, I have sought to continue to reduce the burden of direct taxation – the taxes on income and on capital. My aim is to provide greater rewards for work, enterprise and risk-taking. It also reflects the no less important objective of achieving a better balance between the direct and indirect taxes. Second, as part of the Government's wider policy of improving the supply side of the economy, I have sought to make changes which will improve our economic performance over the long term. My third objective has been to encourage enterprise of all kinds and at all levels. Finally,

> I believe it is of great importance to find ways to make the tax system both simpler to understand and easier to administer.'

He concluded his Budget speech:

> The path of tax reform is never easy, nor the journey free from risk. But, so long as the direction is clear, and the route carefully mapped, the traveller can proceed. My reforms have been guided by two basic principles: the need to make changes that will improve our economic performance over the longer term, and a desire to make life a little simpler for the taxpayer.

134. This strongly suggests that we are reforming *towards* clear objectives, with a strong stress being placed on the incentive and disincentive effects of taxation, and with the objective of simplification as an aim in itself. The national political context of that speech, and others in recent years, was of a need to refocus the system on the economic requirements of incentives.

135. Other comments suggest that we might well be reforming *from* something. As US Secretary to the Treasury James Baker put it (Baker, 1986):

> 'Most ominously, our [US] flawed system threatens our national values. President Reagan recently noted that every time a government begins taxing above a certain level of people's earnings, trust in the government erodes. The belief that others are paying less than their fair share intensifies. Efforts to avoid paying tax spread. Outright cheating, and eventually a distrust and contempt of government itself, follow.
>
> When the United States began our tax reform effort, a poll reflected Americans' deep dissatisfaction with the tax system. According to the survey: 4 of 5 taxpayers believed the tax system benefited the rich and was unfair to the ordinary man or woman; a majority of taxpayers believed the federal income tax system was too complicated; and a majority perceived that cheating on income tax was rampant.
>
> We believe it is of paramount importance that our system be permanently reformed. Halfway efforts must be avoided. We must remember that many of the piecemeal "reforms" of the past are responsible for the problems of today.'

136. The suggestion is that there was a need to regain credibility for the system, and it underlies other comments. The opening passages of the South African Margo Report on reform of taxation make this clear, echoing other comments:

> 'In its report to the President in November 1984 the United States Treasury, under the heading of 'The Need For Tax Reform: Back to Basics', wrote:
>
> > The present income tax is badly in need of fundamental simplification and reform. It is too complicated, it is unfair, and it interferes with economic choices and retards saving, investment and growth . . . The United States income tax is not used simply to raise revenue. Instead, it is used to subsidize a long list of economic activities through exclusions from income subject to tax, adjustments to income, business deductions unrelated to actual expenses, deferral of tax liability, deductions for personal consumption expenditures, tax credits, and preferential tax rates . . .
> >
> > For seven decades, the Treasury Department has fought to protect federal revenues and the fairness and economic neutrality of the tax system from those seeking to create and exploit gaps and inconsistencies in the definition of taxable income. As loopholes have been discovered or created, exploited, and then plugged, techniques of tax avoidance have become increasingly sophisticated and the complexity of the income tax has grown, in a never ending cycle. The resulting tax system is both unfair and needlessly complex. Moreover, it interferes with economic behaviour and, thus, prevents markets from allocating economic resources to their most productive uses. Perhaps worse, the complexity and inequity of the tax system undermine taxpayer morale – a valuable, yet fragile, national asset and a prerequisite for a tax system based on voluntary compliance.'

Tax reform in the Republic [of South Africa] demands, among other things, the restoration of the tax bases, the elimination of erosion and leakages of revenue, the simplification of the structure, the redistribution of the overall tax burden to make it fairer, easier and more acceptable, the modernization of tax systems, the regeneration of taxpayers' confidence in and respect for the fiscus, and the introduction of effective systems of enforcing compliance and of ensuring recovery.'

137. The Australian Draft White Paper on the Reform of the Tax System (June 1985) introduces the subject as follows:

> Few issues touch more people or excite stronger reactions than taxation. Yet, despite a widespread dislike of taxes in all their guises, the demand for government services – which must be financed by taxes – has been increasing for many years. The post-war trend in all advanced countries has been towards the provision of more widespread government services such as pensions, health and education services and community infrastructure. Satisfying those demands has meant that the overall burden of taxation has had to be increased under successive governments . . .
>
> The Government shares the community view that the tax system should be fairer and be seen to be fair. The Australian taxation system traditionally has enjoyed broad taxpayer support but this has obviously waned over the past decade or so. The view is now widespread that the system operates unfairly, impairs economic incentives and is unduly complex. The system is particularly unfair to wage and salary earners at relatively moderate income levels who must pay tax at high marginal rates. Even at high income levels there is unfairness since people with comparable incomes can pay widely different amounts of tax because some are better situated to take advantage of generous tax concessions. The high rates of tax and a tax base riddled with concessions also impairs economic efficiency; it alters people's behaviour and directs resources from their most productive use in the economy. The complexity of the system is notorious. The costs that this complexity impose on taxpayers and tax collectors alike are vexatious to individuals and a deadweight loss to the economy . . . Piecemeal improvements have been made to the system over the years but the point has now been reached where fundamental reforms – rather than further running repairs – are called for.

138. This last, and lengthy, quotation, also shows the extent to which those seeking to reform have watched what has been happening elsewhere closely, and the strength of feeling that the subject engenders. This is also echoed by the phraseology of the opening of the (English language summary of) the Oort Commission's report in the Netherlands :

> 'The 'Queen of taxes' our income tax has been seriously ill for some time now. Over the past few years a procession of physicians has filed past her sickbed. They all agree on the syndrome: she is suffering from excessive complexity. Some even go so far as to declare

the income tax dead; they plead for a worthy successor to the throne in the form of an expenditure tax. Others still detect signs of life. But opinions differ on the best type of cure.

Not only in the Netherlands the income tax is affected by the disease of excessive complexity. In many countries the income tax is bedridden, and attempts are being made to get the patient back on her feet again. The lessons which we can draw from this to remedy the situation in our own country are, however, of limited significance. The medical history of the patients differs too greatly for a useful comparison. International criticism of the income tax does confirm the diagnosis that it is a serious ailment. When only a small minority of people are able to fill in their tax return without help, there is something fundamentally wrong.'

139. Similar comments could be drawn from reports and reviews from many other states. Something had gone wrong the way taxing machinery had developed to the point at which taxpayer intolerance was becoming politically significant. There was a need to reassess what the systems were actually doing.

140. That need to reassess coincided, it is suggested, with four separate circumstances, all of which influenced the process of reform. First, and one to note rather than explore, is that the levels of inflation in the leading economies were much more comfortable in the early 1980s than they had been in the immediate past period – and optimistic views suggested they might stay that way, even though events in some major economies have since shown that view to be very optimistic. However, there was a window during which tax systems which bore the scars of the inflation effects in distorting the alignments and balances of systems could be adjusted without further immediate distortion from the same cause.

141. Secondly, there has been a shift – of which the 'tax revolt' as it was termed in some places was part – away from the role of the state as provider to the role of the state as arbiter. This is of course most dramatically seen in the dismantling of the hard-line socialism in Poland and Hungary and the moves to *perestroika* in the USSR. Throughout Europe socialist or social-democrat governments fell from power, or became more market-oriented in their approaches. The *Economist* recently summarised it thus:

> 'As in America, neo-conservatism's time has come. Belief in a benign, interventionist state was badly shaken ... Taxpayers, especially, though not only, middle-income ones, were fed up. Welfare capitalism seemed to have hit a limit.' (Economist, 1989).

142. Third, the systems were growing increasingly interactive with other national economies. This is a major factor because, as the Dutch report noted, the directions in which national reforms occur cannot be expected to be the same, even given the international nature of the political shifts in opinions, except insofar as international pressures force conformity on national reforms.

143. It is in this latter aspect that the reform movement of the last few years is different from measures that have been taken before. The importance of this, as seen by smaller states - particularly those with open economies – was spelt out in 1990 when the Belgian authorities confronted the problems of reform. This high taxed state came relatively late to reforms, partly because of the need to find an internal political consensus. As a result it found its options curbed by international tax competition. One result was a letter of protest to the IMF and an appeal for action to stop these pressures because they were in danger of being overwhelmed by them. This competition is a major theme of our study, and is the fourth of the factors.

144. This point is made strongly in the recent Canadian White Paper introducing the final stage of Canadian tax reform, *Goods and Services Tax: An Overview*.

> Canada's prospects for economic growth in the future are rooted in the steps we take today. in a world in which change occurs quickly, our ability to respond to that change,m to take advantage of the opportunities it presents, determines our ability to safeguard the economic security of all Canadians . . . In today's international marketplace, an important factor in determining a country's ability to compete successfully is the efficiency with which it uses its resources . . .
>
> However the efficient use of . . . resource has been hampered by our reliance on an outdated, discriminatory and unreliable federal sales tax . . . Canada is now the only industrialised country in the world that continues to impose a tax on sales by manufacturers. The present manufacturer's sales tax is antiquated and harmful to the Canadian economy . . . Because of the way the present tax is structures, Canada's exports are subject to a hidden tax and are more costly to produce than comparable products from other countries.'

145. It was perhaps not so surprising, given that statement, that the proposed new Canadian tax was one based closely on developments elsewhere.

Objectives

146. The widespread shift in political attitudes was bound to reflect into the objectives of tax reforms which were, partly for other unrelated reasons, increasingly felt to be necessary, although the remarks quoted above suggest that the extent to which the reform was led by a positive re-alignment of objectives, rather than a need to reform itself causing the reformers to seek objectives, varies from one state to another to quite a degree. And, as always, even within one system the objectives are often irreconcilable.

147. The Australian Government made perhaps one of the clearest statements of objectives in its 1985 reform proposals, where it set out the following 'principles':

> 'First, there must be no increase in the overall tax burden, as measured by the shares of Commonwealth Government tax revenue in gross domestic product through the Government's current term office.
>
> Second, any reform must continue the process already begun by the Government, and provide further cuts in personal income tax.
>
> Third, taxation changes must contribute to smashing tax avoidance and evasion, which remain as features of the tax system which the Government inherited.
>
> Fourth, any reform must lead to a simpler system, which therefore all Australians can understand more easily, and which therefore makes tax avoidance and evasion more difficult.
>
> Fifth, any reform package must result in a tax system which is fairer so that Australians are only required to pay tax according to their capacity to pay, and the overall system must be progressive.
>
> Sixth, any tax reform must not disadvantage recipients of welfare benefits, and should reduce or remove "poverty traps"
>
> Seventh, if any reform package which includes changes in indirect taxes is contemplated, it must be acceptable to the various groups

in the Australian community whose response will determine whether we can maintain moderation in wage movements.

Eighth, any reform must provide the best possible climate for investment, growth and employment in Australia.

Ninth, any reform package must have widespread community support, including support at a widely representative National Taxation Summit of economic organizations and community groups.'

148. There is a noticeable shift away in this statement, which is stated in other forms in other states (as with the Belgian Royal Commission, or the Irish Commission), from the sentiment which flavoured the thinking of the famous Canadian Carter Commission on taxation two decades before, which regarded the first aim of taxation as sharing fairly the burden of the state between taxpayers. Is the once prevalent idea that taxation was, above all, about redistribution of the nation's wealth, now no longer an aim?

Redistribution

149. The systems we had in most developed states before the present waves of changes were the creations of war or seige economies building on taxes developed earlier this century. These had then been extended or altered to suit the moods of the 1960s when we recovered from the shocks of war to the benefits of the social state, a movement combined with a quadrupling in the numbers of individual states as ex-colonies became independent throughout the world. Those new states – and the not-so-new states of South America too – frequently adopted by imitation systems used by the imperial powers if not in detail, at least in concept. And where direct imitation did not happen, indirect imitation occurred as the requirements of national and international bankers and their consultants applied other pressures to the same ends.

150. In the last few years those earlier attitudes have been doubted. A concern with egalitarianism has changed to a concern with neutrality. Whilst that might sound like tautology, its significance to a tax system is profound. The social ideal is for the redistribution of wealth, and that demands taxes which make the state rich, so that it can dispense its largesse, or which transfer funds more directly from the wealthier to the poorer. It is, above all, concerned with what is termed by economists vertical equity – that the system is 'fair' between those with different economic resources.

151. It may be that this concern with equality arose from those same pressures of war that caused our taxes to rise – or from the pressures that, in part, lay behind the wars and revolutions of half a century ago. Historians have many opinions on this. What we can discern is the assumption that we needed to use our tax systems to redistribute income or wealth required progressive taxes. Two taxes were at hand : the personal income tax and the estate or inheritance duty. Both were widely used.

152. Whilst this might have satisfied politicians and voters, economists increasingly pointed out that the redistribution was an illusion – the taxes did not do what it was said they would do. Musgrave, in *Fiscal Systems*, a seminal work, pointed that out in 1969. It was for social security systems to redistribute, if that is what the government wanted.

153. Furthermore, once the accepted wisdom was challenged, its weaknesses were revealed. As Sandford reminded us in his comments on tax reform nearly two decades ago (Sandford, 1971):

> The unanswerable question is: "What degree of progression?" As Goschen put it in the debate on the estate duty of 1894, when progression was first consistently applied to a British tax:
>
> "When you embark on this system of graduation there are no stages, no landmarks, nothing whatever to guide you. There is no principle of justice – no principle, where you can say you ought to stop; no principle of prudence – no principle whatever. Equality of sacrifice will not find correspondence in the geometrical progression of taxation . . . You have attempted an impossibility if you attempt to reach what is real equality of sacrifice."

Neutrality

154. At the same time as some disillusion was spreading about the efficacy of our main taxes, other pressures were building up, as the political mood changed. Our objective now is to be neutrality, with taxes that do not penalise one person rather than another. They give equality of opportunity, rather than equality of result. The ideal tax is one that takes from us in proportion to what we have, or what we use, in such a way that the tax affects our behavioural patterns to the minimum. This is a concern for horizontal equality. A 'fair' tax is one which presents us with a 'level playing field' and does not concern itself with the quality of the teams. It is for them to undertake their own training if they wish to win.

155. This shifting appears to be occurring now to an extent few could

have foretold a few years ago. As we move in Europe to the post-1992 Single European market, and within it to currency union and the 'Schengen' frontier-free area, so the barrier with the other half of Europe appears to be crumbling fast, so that the social centralised economies of the USSR, Czecho-slovakia, Hungary and Poland, at least, are adjusting to reflect these same ideas of neutrality rather than equity. As the movement widens, so it strengthens itself, and exposes more those who have not adjusted.

156. And again, whilst there are leaders an imitators in the field, so some who might have wished to stand aside will feel the pressures of the bankers and advisers, of bodies like the IMF and the World Bank, to reform as, for example, Kenya has done recently.

157. The aim of neutrality argues for lower marginal rates of tax and tax bases which are comprehensive with few tax expenditures or exceptions. It is the broad direction of much recent tax reform of direct taxes.

Other objectives

158. Even as this chapter was written, it would seem the political equation will move again. The developed world, having enjoyed an unprecedented four decades of peace within its boundaries, has discovered that, rather than destroying each other, we are all together destroying ourselves. 1989 saw governments for the first time starting to grapple seriously with the problems of the environment, and finding taxes have a role to play here as well.

159. Taxation provides one answer to the issue of pollution and the despoiling of our natural resources. It occurs as one way of implementing the OECD's polluter-pays principle. How do you make the polluter pay or, in other terms, how is the producer of a product to be made to bear the external costs of his product as well as the direct costs? How can the consumer be made to accept that his consumption, say, of this book or a daily newspaper, involves the desertification of areas affected by felled trees, with a loss of rain forest? And that the light by which the book is read is causing the burning of non-renewable energy resources? Specific taxes provide one of the easier answers to this issue. But does that not run directly contrary to the aim of neutrality? And who is to benefit from the tax collected – the next generation rather than this? Nonetheless, the taxation system is being recruited as one technique among others to distort the market in favour of those using renewable resource and against those using products with higher external costs than market prices.

160. The targeting of this kind of tax is in the area of the indirect taxes and those payments in the grey area between taxes and charges. There is a definitional problem here. If you pay for what you get, it is a charge, if you pay for what I get, it is a tax. If when buying what you want to get, you are obliged to pay also for what I am forced to get, is that a tax or a charge? Within the definition of this study, it is a tax, but for others it may be best presented as a user charge.

161. Another issue is also having a growing effect on the actions of tax authorities and those with whom they cooperate. This is the 'war' against drugs. This argument can take many forms. It is strongly argued by some that the present attempt to control drugs by criminal laws is failing – and that whole economies are being distorted with the illegal moneys resulting. Far better, they say, to legalise it and then tax it, like alcohol or tobacco, two of the western world's major revenue earners for governments.

162. By contrast, others argue that the weak points of the current international tax system – tax havens and shelters – are also useful to conceal the illegal proceeds of drug businesses. One way, they urge, to tackle the drug problem is to tackle money flows resulting from it. This means a much tougher approach to suspect flows of money – and thereby the drugs effort and the effort of a state against tax evaders become the same effort.

163. These last points are raised not to express any views upon them, but to illustrate the instability of the aims of any set of reforms. Taxation is but one of the ways in which governments control their people (or, in democracies, the people control themselves), as is the criminal law or the law of civil liability (either of which provide other answers to the pollution problem). The trend in recent years has been to prevent tax influencing people either in intended or unintended ways by removing distortions, for example in the savings market, and to reduce the use of incentives in taxation. Perhaps future trends will be to reimpose distortions both in favour of and against conduct subject to prevalent political attitudes. Perhaps our tax systems will go 'green'. If so, it must be asked whether that will interfere with the achievements of the present reforms.

164. I believe, and argue below, that some features of the present changes will not go away. They will provide a new system which will no doubt be adapted to other forms. But the shifts that are occurring will have long term effects. The reasons for the permanence lie in part with other issues involved in the present round of tax reform rather than the political objectives behind them, and in part with that very inertia which, as is charted

in the next chapter, has caused change to be slow in progress in many countries.

Simplicity

165. A 'gut feeling' appears in many states that the existing tax laws are too complicated. They are too expensive to comply with and too difficult to administer. We saw above that this was the way it was put in the opening paragraph of the 1984 US Treasury Report to the President: 'The present US tax system desperately need simplification and reform. It is too complicated . . .' Very similar thoughts were echoed by the Dutch Oort Commission and formed part of the political arguments for reform in other states. It has several times been used to support British reform measures. It is one of the Australian 'ninc principles'. The Belgian Royal Commission confined itself to six objectives and again simplicity was one. Its importance was stressed thus (Betten, 1987):

> 'The transparency of a tax system is an indispensible prerequisite to the success of a tax reform plan. The tax system should be simple and comprehensive in its structure and application. A simple structure insures efficient levying of taxes and reduces errors, disputes and tax avoidance possibilities. The simplicity of a tax system contributes to its legal stability. Inconsistent interpretations of the law, possibilities of creating exceptions, disparities between the legal text and its practical application all make correct application of the law more difficult and lead to emigration, searches for tax avoidance mechanisms and simple fraud.'

166. How is simplicity achieved? One test is itself simple: weigh the text of the national laws – the lighter the better; there is less to understand, get wrong, administer, etc. Another test is to reduce administrators' decisions, and therefore the number of administrators. A third – though one less likely to be attempted – is to make the laws more comprehensible to the average taxpayer. A fourth is to leave less room for argument by taxpayers about intent and meaning.

167. A genuine simplification will meet to some extent all these targets. The laws will be more straightforward, clearer, easier to understand, less open to argument, doubt and appeals to the courts, and subject to fewer exceptions. But attempts at this objective have – largely – failed. Witness the complications of the US Tax Reform Act and the 'Technical Corrections Act' which had to follow it. Witness also the UK Finance Acts of 1986 and 1989, or the statutes required to back reforms in Canada,

Australia and Ireland. I am not able to judge how far this extends in other languages, although translations of texts suggest the problems are the same.

168. Simplification runs contrary to two powerful factors: justice and comprehensiveness. The easiest way to simplify is to adopt broad-sweeping provisions, and remove the minor exceptions and special cases. This gives rise promptly both to political pressures from those who secured the original special legislation, and from the revenue authorities keen not to let tax funds escape through the 'minor' transactions omitted from broadly drawn tax bases.

169. Attempts to avoid the second problem – tax avoidance – in a legislatively simple way gives rise to other problems. Attempts at a totally comprehensive direct tax base couched in 'simple' terms tends to mean draconian legislation. If so, then another of the Smithian aims of taxation is traversed – that of certainty. Commentaries suggest that this is the price paid for some of the new provisions.

170. Nonetheless, 'simplicity' is an aim with political appeal, and it has undoubtedly led to the scrapping of some aspects of tax systems – for example, the multi-rate schedules many states had for imposing income tax. Once stated as an aim, it is also a useful argument to prevent governments adding too many further new special provisions.

171. There is also another route to simplicity – rate reduction. If the marginal rate of taxes are halved, and the distinctions between the rates applied to different taxes (such as income and capital gains) are removed or reduced, the complications have a much lower economic price. Whilst they are not removed physically, they cease to matter so much economically.

172. Another approach is to shift the tax burden from the inherently more complicated taxes to the simpler ones. Alternatively, or at the same time, tax can be shifted from those taxes which will be disputed to those which will not. This is a subjective, psychological, matter. But it is observable that throughout the developed world governments are able to operate rules for their social security taxes that would be less acceptable and more readily challenged politically and legally if they were non-earmarked taxes. Each of those trends is present in national reforms, as is demonstrated below.

International aspects of reform

173. What has been sidestepped in most of the reports and discussions so far is the international aspect of tax reform. By that I mean the international interaction of systems, not the relative national competitiveness or 'differentness' of systems which have been shown clearly to be in the minds of reformers. Little of the literature has expressly addresed the question, and much of the political debate has been couched in purely national terms. Attention was paid to other states, as already noted, to ensure that one's own system was competitive. It is only as the momentum of the reform movement has grown that states have started to become concerned with the end result for them.

174. This absence of earlier attention (at least, on the record) does not unduly surprise. Apart from the United States, rather less attention is paid to double tax treaties than internal laws. Those states which were concerned had systems which to quite an extent neutralised international double direct taxation. Others were prepared to forego the problems of international taxation.

175. Yet the background to the reforms suggests that international aspects should play a much greater role in any state's view of its tax systems than has hitherto been the case. This is particularly so within the member States of the European Community, as all of them are aware. But the trend is much wider. GATT and World Bank figures both show that international trade of states is growing far faster than national GDPs. GATT figures show that world trade in manufactured goods has risen at between two and three times the speed of growth of manufacturing output since 1960, and total imports and exports grow steadily faster than GDP in many states.

176. Exports of services and of capital have also grown. Both are a reflection of the liberalisation of world trade, to which GATT has slowly been working, and both also reflect the liberalisation of capital markets which has been another recent trend, as the 1989 World Bank's World Development Report notes:

> Many high-income countries have eased their capital controls and cut restrictions on the entry of foreign intermediaries . . . offshore financial markets have grown much more quickly than domestic markets in recent years . . . these changes . . . are likely to prove irreversible.

177. It follows that growing sectors of the economies of major states are to a growing extent part of the international as much as the national economic system. How have tax reforms taken this into account, and what effects have reforms had upon it? The comments of two American observers are worth repeating.

178. Summers, writing in 1988, commented:

> Until recently, international taxation has been an arcane subspecialty among American tax lawyers, and international considerations have rarely influenced the thrust of tax reform. Instead, tax rules have been crafted in consultation with domestic interests; tax incentives have been instituted to spur American individuals and companies to work toward perceived national goals; and the overall level of tax collections has been determined on the basis of American business conditions. Such a provincial approach to tax policy may have been appropriate in an earlier era, but the increasing economic integration of the world requires a more global approach to tax policy. The emphasis in recent American tax reform debates on competitiveness is only a precursor to a time in which international considerations will play a pervasive role in shaping tax policies.
>
> If nations pursue tax policies without regard to international objectives, the result will inevitably be economic conflict. Competition among nations will make it difficult to effectively tax multinational companies, and inconsistent policies toward saving and investment will give rise to disruptive trade imbalances.

179. Writing the same year, Dodge and Sargent noted the inevitable effect of the US reforms on other states:

> The impact of the 1986 U.S. tax reforms on pressures for international tax harmonization is one of the more interesting analytic issues connected with these reforms. The impact of the 1986 reform package goes far beyond the effect of the reductions in statutory tax rates, though the rate reductions have by themselves had a powerful effect. Structural changes in the taxation of international income of U.S. companies have increased tax harmonization pressures.
>
> Perhaps the most interesting effect of the U.S. reforms is that they have increased the pressure to harmonize statutory as well as effective tax rates, thus greatly increasing the constraints faced by desig-

ners of tax reform in other countries. Before 1986, international tax arbitrage opportunities created by differentials in statutory tax rates were important, but their constraining effect on tax policy was diluted by the existence of other tax minimisation practices open to U.S. companies with international operations. For example, the LIFO rule used under pre-1986 U.S. tax law in allocating foreign taxes to income distributed to U.S. parents permitted multinational corporations with growing foreign operations to minimize total taxes worldwide by paying dividends in alternate years, concentrating foreign deductions that were more generous than corresponding U.S. deductions in those years in which dividends were not paid.

180. How can those perceptions be related to the political structure of the world as it is ? This dilemma is central to any continuing process of reform. It is summed up in the following way by two of the world's leading commentators on tax structures:

'Differences in tax systems did not come about at random, but rather reflect social and political preferences that should not be ignored' (Cnossen, 1986)

'On the whole, then, I see no reason to alter my conclusion of a decade ago (Bird 1976) that those interested in taxation in developing countries would be well advised to pay more attention to the details of the particular countries in which they are concerned and less to largely irrelevant international tax comparisons.' (Bird 1988).

181. If the effect of the pressures of reform is to remove the scope for those preferences, and for accommodating the details of particular nations, what is the effect on those preferences and details, and on those characteristics by which we differentiate states?

Chapter 2

Trends in national reforms

Digo, paciencia y barajar
(I say – patience, and shuffle the cards)
Cervantes, Don Quixote

200. This chapter draws on the materials noted in the previous chapter, and research into the changes that have taken place in the world's major economies and a selection of other states, to suggest the patterns of reform (if, indeed, there are tendencies strong enough to be called patterns) emerging in differing states. It is a firm conclusion that there are such patterns, though these are not always the intended shape originally planned, nor does it follow that they achieve the objectives that dynamised the reform process. Nor, and this must be noted also, are the actual reforms the same as those that are presented as occurring – or not occurring.

A new Age of Reform

201. The first, and most fundamental, proposition is that there has been a near-universal move to tax reform. The title 'New Age of Reform' was offered in a public lecture to the Institute for Fiscal Studies by David Henderson, head of the economics section at the OECD (published in Fiscal Studies, 1989). Henderson compares the present move towards economic liberalism, of which he sees the tax reforms as part, with the Gladstonian era in Britain. Although the analogy is national, he emphasises, in a way fully borne out by events, that the move towards reform is universal and has occurred around the globe.

202. This universality is important for a number of reasons. First, it means that such moves are considered appropriate – or necessary – regardless of the political, developmental or constitutional position in any one state. The importance of that proposition should not be underestimated. For example, viewed from the domestic scene of the United Kingdom, it is easy to accept that the tax reforms in this country in the 1980's were 'Thatcherism'. They are, after all, what was said by many political commentators to have secured the Thatcher government election and reelection. It comes as a revelation to some to find that those same meas-

ures which have secured political popularity in Britain for a conservative government secured similar successes for governments of radically different political persuasions elsewhere.

Why reform should not occur

203. The universality is important to emphasise also because it appears to refute an argument put forward by political scientists suggesting that tax reform does *not* take place. The argument is that 'an old tax is a good tax' from the point of view of the legislator of taxes. This was put strongly by Professor Richard Rose of the Centre for the Study of Public Policy in the University of Strathclyde in a paper in 1985 ('Maximising tax revenue whilst minimising political cost: Journal of Public Policy, vol 5) and expanded to book length in 1987 (*Taxation by Political Inertia*, R Rose and T Karran).

204. In a challenging section, Rose summarises his theory thus:

> The future of taxation is already here; it has been delivered by the inertia of the past. Most taxes that will be in force in the year 2001 are already on the statute books. Most tax laws of future importance were decided generations or centuries ago. Political inertia ensures that the bulk of public revenue at the start of the next millenium will depend much more on old laws than upon new ones.

205. He develops this argument in the same chapter (What scope for future change?) in a section headed 'Constraints upon reform'. He argues that tax reforms are all very well when issued from the mouths or pens of theorists or even opposition politicians, but that the realities are far from this, with little decisive reform. Why? Partly because the system has to start from its existing defects and cannot begin again. If the transition between the present system and the desired end is too expensive or difficult, then the desired end must be forgotten.

206. Another major constraint is that of electoral politics. Rose quotes Richard Goode's rule of thumb that in any reform beneficiaries must outnumber losers by four to one, because losers will always shout louder than winners. Linked with this is the need to find the finance for a tax reform, in order to avoid adverse criticism. To be welcomed, they should reduce taxation, but this can only be done within the context of the overall budgetary requirements of the state. When (as is almost always the case) governments are revenue-hungry, tax reforms are going to receive low priority. This links also to the next factor Rose identifies. This final constraint is administrative politics. Changes are costly administratively.

They are unpredictable, and are therefore not welcomed by those required to put them into effect.

Why reform occurs

207. Why, then, in Rose's view, do changes occur? Rose wrote his work after the Tax Reform Act of 1986, and the shifts in the United Kingdom up to that time, and was clearly aware of them. His answer is that 'in the fullness of time, the destabilising effects of political inertia can introduce big net changes that politicians have not consciously chosen . . . The cause of change is usually not the discovery of new ideas about taxation, but political changes that make the costs of doing nothing much greater than a decision to act. For example, VAT was not introduced because it had suddenly been invented. Antecedents of the tax had been used in past centuries . . . The only changes that can be expected are strictly incremental changes in the rate and base of existing taxes, and other elements of fringe tuning.'
This, he quotes the well-known British commentator Cedric Sandford as concluding, is 'a pretty pitiful result from two decades of enthusiastic tax reform' (C Sandford and A Robinson, *Tax policy-making in the United Kingdom*, 1983).

208. Rose's work, and that of those he quotes, contains important insights, the results of which surface regularly in national reforms. Australian reforms, the first time around, ran into trouble because an attempt was made for a most ambitious consensus of national opinion through a national tax conference. Similarly in Japan, where consensus is much more the order of all major changes, tax reform waited upon financial and sex scandals before squeezing through – and even then brought upon its progenitors the wrath of the nation's housewives. In Germany and Canada the problem arises from a federal constitutional structure where the federal government has to work with the provincial governments if reforms are to succeed. And in Canada, as in the USSR, tax issues may become woven into constitutional issues of the balance of powers between state and regions. In South Africa, amongst other countries, reforms which were felt right were – it was felt more powerfully – too expensive. It is significant that in South Africa, and in other states (Belgium is another example) where it was felt that reform could wait, it waited only two or three years. This is against the context that in just about every state apart from the United Kingdom even tax-neutral reforms were hard to afford unless the extra tax needed could be found elsewhere.

209. At the same time, Rose reflects to some extent the naivety likely in

the average voter in his view that there was nothing new about VAT, or that a little trimming of rates and bases does not constitute a serious reform. It may be so for the average voter that his total average tax burden does not change much – how can it unless there are major changes in the need for public finance? But the effect on the average business may be much sharper, as may the change in the administrative requirements.

210. This naivety is itself very important to Rose's assumptions. But it is not, with respect, relevant to most of those concerned with the major thrust of tax reform in the last decade. These are people who can afford good advice and know precisely what is or is not taxed. To them a 'marginal' rate cut of 5% is of major significance. They are also, increasingly, people not tied unduly closely to any one tax system. They, or their goods, services or capital, can cross frontiers with increasing ease, by jet, freight, telephone, or telegraphic transfer. Their residences can move, or they can choose to work through corporate subsidiaries anywhere they wish.

211. As a result of this, imperceptibly perhaps, another factor has entered the political analysis. Tax systems used once – almost – to be solely decided by a nation. Now even the biggest economies have tax systems which are part of the same world economy, and they are in competition together. This is not just that where the United States goes, there also probably goes Canada; it is that countries like the Netherlands have done well by being highly competitive in their tax regimes, and they intend to stay that way. And it is that if a state like the United Kingdom tax foreign executives at 83%, they will probably base themselves in a country with a rate of 50% – or one with a tax holiday for them. If states do not take note of this, much of the financial flows and trade now going through, say, Rotterdam and Amsterdam might just go somewhere else. The national system is, then, caught between being in the political home market place and the financial world market place.

212. States are increasingly aware of this. At first, awareness came to the first small tax haven states – colonies of the United Kingdom and the Netherlands – who came to be tax havens almost by accident (for example, the British Virgin Islands), or, as with Switzerland, where laws introduced for other purposes became useful also for tax purposes. Since then, it has developed with deliberate changes of tax and non-tax laws to build sophisticated machinery to support tax haven status. Witness the elaborate corporate laws of a country such as the Cayman Islands, with no tax system; or the adoption of trust laws by a country such as Liechtenstein to which otherwise the concept is alien; or the recent changes on such matters as bank secrecy in Malta, as it deliberately realigns its structures to become a successful competitor in the world market for low tax countries.

213. Another variant, to which many much larger states have succumbed is the niche marketing of tax systems. Luxembourg has developed a specialism in mutual fund (unit trust or UCITS) taxation so successful that when the European Community opened the Community market for mutual funds, the United Kingdom was forced to make major cuts in both rate and base in the way it taxed the funds. Singapore has developed specialist banking competence. Ireland is the home of the ten per cent company. And the united States were early contenders with the controversial Domestic International Sales Corporations. Even the USSR, it seems, is learning the art of onshore 'offshore' zones with its proposals to develop tourism in the Black Sea areas by just such tax regimes.

214. The importance of this latter factor is also borne out by the course national reforms have taken. Some states – for example the Netherlands, Belgium, Australia, Canada – have openly argued national reform for international competitiveness. Others, such as the smaller states, have little option. Where others lead, they must follow.

215. The double pressure is, perhaps, one of the main problems to be resolved by any tax reform. Unless the voters will support the tax policy – and pay the taxes – the government in a genuine democracy will be out. At the same time, an international free for all in the tax market place will send rates spiralling down, and tax bases will be narrowed by successive concessions. Fiscal deficits will grow until the process is forced into reverse.

216. The cost of stepping out of line may itself be high. There can be no clearer example than that of the abortive attempt by the Federal German government to impose a withholding tax on savings. The tax, in 1988-89, lasted six months, and was then repealed. It was soon gone, but its effects, the IMF has noted, may last much longer. The mobility of savings ensured that funds were shifted to where no withholdings were applied. Competition ensured that local banks as well as outsiders competed for these funds. Mark-denominated financial instruments became available that did not previously exist. And when the pressure was removed, the newfound expertise and opportunities remained, so only part of the 'missing' funds were repatriated. The lesson is clear. If attempting to go against the pressures of the reform programme is too expensive for Germany, who else can argue?

Why has reform occurred?

217. What we cannot finally tell, but must guess, is whether what we are seeing is a passing phase on such a cyclical process or contains changes

which will have permanent effect. My belief is that because of this international element to all recent national changes, part of the process will not be reversible in likely political circumstances. This is compounded because of underlying demographic shifts, administrative techniques and other factors noted below which, whilst still new, will be long term in their effects. it is also because, as is argued later, that the kind of system to which states are shifting is more stable than that from which they are shifting, making a reversal of reforms less likely than their development. It is strengthened by the extent to which states and individuals both monitor each other's thoughts and progress. A series of symposia on tax reform, such as those held in 1987 by the Brookings Institute and by France with the OECD, and the following year by the University of Virginia, compound and strengthen the process they seek to monitor.

218. We looked in Chapter 1 at the question Why Reform Now? and noted a number of separate influences at work. It is beyond the scope of this study – and perhaps too premature in any event – to trace the full story of the reasoning behind the changes that have taken place, although it would – and will – make more sense of the process when that is done. Clearly some states took a lead. One must be the United States, where the openness of government to the ideas of the theorists coincided with a 'revolution' as some termed it against high taxes (by which is usually meant high rates of direct tax). Another must be the United Kingdom where tax reform again was motivated by an internal need for 'lower' tax, and affected by special factors – the availability of petroleum taxes and the value added tax to take up the slack. Others resisted, like the refusal twice by the plebiscite in Switzerland to support VAT in the 1970's and, less directly, the inability of the Japanese government to secure any consensus for its proposed reforms or the refusal of the Norwegian people to join the European Communities in 1972. Yet – at the time of writing – all three of those states are reconsidering the wisdom of earlier stubbornness.

219. Theorists donated some powerful ideas to the debate. One is the Laffer curve. It is self-evident, so it was argued, that if a tax rate is zero, no tax will be collected, and if the tax rate is 100%, then again no tax will be collected because noone will pay it. There must therefore be some midpoint at which a maximum amount of tax can be collected. It follows that you may raise taxes by cutting the rate, if your present tax rate is too high. Recent expert academic thought has started to cast doubt on the existence of a curve from zero to zero via an optimal high point, but the idea has already worked, or so it seems.

220. Particularly in the United States, they also argued cogently for clean, simple, comprehensive taxes, as the papers in the Symposium on Tax Reform published by *Economic Perspectives* in Summer 1987 shows.

221. Another idea is attributable to Stanley Surrey – the Tax Expenditure. Starting from the assumption of a comprehensive base of any tax, he argued, then any exception from that base represents a loss to the Treasury. Such a loss is a public expenditure, just as if the government had decided to collect the tax and then spend it on the same objectives. Since this idea surfaced, it has been discussed by the OECD, and has become common practice in some states to publish regular lists of tax expenditures. Once quantified in this way, loopholes and exemptions from tax become harder to defend and easier for a government looking for extra revenue to abolish. The popularity of this idea has coincided with a growth in the competence of governments to measure quantitatively what they are doing. Their information may still be imperfect, but tax reforms no longer rely on hunches and intuition in the way they did. Nor can politicians quite so easily fool others – and themselves – that things are a good idea if quantitatively they do not work.

222. This idea has been taken up widely by member states of the OECD, and has discussed by them collectively. Lists of tax expenditures have also been included in national revenue statistics by a number of states. Applying the idea at its logical extent, the Oort Commission in the Netherlands appended to its report a review of the consequences of removing all expenditures from its tax system. The result was a reduction of rates at all levels by two or three percentage points. This is because, as Swaine observed in 1987 comparing the US and UK corporate taxes, the width of bases and extent of allowances varies markedly from one country to another. Even after reforms, some state still have narrower tax bases than others which have not changed their systems. The idea, nonetheless, is powerful.

223. These simple ideas are supported by a much higher level of competence generally to examine the economics of taxation, and to test theories in practice, all which has led to clearer thinking about the reasons for tax. A recent volume published for the World Bank chronicles this process for developing states: Newbury's *The Theory of Taxation in Developing States*. Perhaps as a result politicians have been a little less free to pronounce upon the 'justice' of tax systems, and a little more ready to concede the unintended economic side-effects of well-meant reforms in the past.

224. There were clearly many other factors at play – as Henderson's paper suggests. And there were lucky breaks too, like Britain's North Sea oil, and the fact that the reform ideas were gathering pace during a period of economic expansion in many states coupled with low inflation rates. A United States President who saw at first hand the taxpayer revolt in California was serving at the time that many leaders looked at ever-rising public expenditure and at their popularity, and felt the former had to slow down. There is the steadily increasing convergence of the member states of the European Communities, and the growth of shared official experience through this, the OECD and other international bodies.

225. 'Reform', it is suggested, is not one single movement or process, but a number of developments which, for varying reasons, have coincided within a climate of change favourable politically, economically and administratively. Whilst that is true of the processes, the results have converged. The changes that occurred are two-fold in nature : changes between taxes and changes within taxes.

Changing the tax balance

226. A major factor in current changes is the growing awareness of past and future growth in the largest element in community expenditure in many states – the cost of social welfare programmes. This itself has no one explanation – the growing costs of a growing retired population, growing health care costs and declining numbers of people at work are partial explanations. Nor is it new. The OECD held an important, if not widely noticed, seminar in 1981 on the coming crisis of the 90s. Its concern was a more short term one – how the expanding programmes of the '50s and '60s could be financed within the – it was anticipated – straitened budgets of the '80s and '90s. The economic predictions were on the pessimistic side, but the quandary is real enough.

227. Nor is there any one answer – partly because states have adopted fundamentally different approaches to financing their social security systems. The traditional answer developed first in Germany of compulsory insurance through private insurers is one answer. At the other extreme, an answer is to fund expenditure through general taxation without special measures, as in Australasia.

228. The absence of special taxes or user charges is, to date, an unusual way: adopted in Australia and New Zealand and to a limited extent in the Netherlands. Denmark also has a low contribution level. It is a response, however, to the fact that such expenditure may now be the larger part of

public expenditure in a state – in a sense *all* taxes are in large part social security taxes. It is also a response to administrative complexity if, as is increasingly the case, user charges for compulsory insurance are income based. For example, a person employed on average pay in Britain is paying two income taxes based on his earnings : at 25% and 9%, whilst the employer is paying a payroll tax on the same base of 10.45%. In France, a similar picture emerges, except that the social security charges are much higher in aggregate than the income tax charges, as they are in the Netherlands because little of the cost of social security is traditionally borne by general taxation. In both states the income from social security taxes now forms 43% of total tax income. Yet in France, the social security funds are under enormous pressure and have had to be subsidised from general taxation, just as in the Netherlands part of the burden has now been transferred to general taxation.

229. In most developed states, where there are separate social security premiums/taxes, the relative importance of social security funding has increased. Austria, Belgium, Netherlands, Canada, Switzerland, Greece and the UK all show that taxation collected from social security sources is a rising share of total taxation, whilst taxation is also absorbing a rising share of GDP. In all the OECD states apart from Luxembourg and, marginally, Turkey social security contributions were a larger share of GDP in 1985 than they were in 1980, (and only in Italy, Norway and the UK were the 1980 shares lower than in 1975. The unweighted averages over the period were:
1970: 5.9%; 1975: 7.7%; 1980: 8.6%; 1985: 9.2%

230. The latest available figure, for 1987, shows the total still rising at 9.5%. As a result, contributions are usually a greater share of total taxes, in individual states in recent years. In states where the share of taxes taken by social security have declined (Italy, Spain, Portugal), it is against backgrounds of particularly sharp rises in the share of GDP taken in taxation (from 30% to 36% in Italy). Interestingly, the real growth in share of total taxes occurred between 1970 and 1975 (about 4%) rising only slowly and uncertainly since then.

231. This increase has been effected by various measures, for example all OECD states bar the UK, Ireland and Greece levy social security taxes on fringe benefits (and the states without social security taxes are, coincidentally, the ones attacking fringe benefits with special taxes). Rates have risen in a number of states, and the base of the tax is usually broad – based on full earnings, rather than earnings net of expenses. It would suggest that there is less room for erosion of tax bases by allowances or avoidance in social security taxation than in ordinary direct taxes, making the taxes

more buoyant as earnings rise. There is also an absence of arrangements parallel to foreign tax credits in potential double tax cases. The figures also suggest that the social security reforms of the base – usually involving transferring the funding from a premium basis to an income related basis – took place some time ago, and were made buoyant by subsequent wage inflation, although some states have eased up rates more recently.

232. This easing reflects a growing concern in these states with the highest levels of earmarked social security funding that their systems are becoming uncompetitive. Such concerns are now expressed about the very high levels of employer-borne French social security charges. The dilemma of the newly democratised central European states may be even sharper. Hungary's payroll costs are 65% of earnings and fund a social security system made more expensive by the (by international standards) low general retirement age of 62. Can that be afforded now that Hungary is forced to compete in the international labour market, or is that (thinking of the quotations at the end of chapter 1) a detail that will have to go?

The direct – indirect balance

233. The division, implicit in the European Community treaties and in many discussions, between direct taxes (the income and property taxes) and indirect taxes (those on goods and services), may be weak in theory, but is one to which attention is often paid at the political level. In the period prior to current reform, it has been felt by some that the balance had been shifting so that greater shares of tax were collected by direct taxes.

234. In some states (the United Kingdom and, most recently, Canada are examples) conscious decisions have been made to shift the weight of taxation back on to indirect taxes from direct taxes. Even so, there have been few major changes in balance in the last 20 years in the developed states (though they are happening as other states become more developed, such as South Korea and Hungary). In a number of states there were changes between 1965 and 1975 as goods and services taxes declined and were overtaken in tax share by social security taxation: Belgium, France, Germany, Italy, Japan, Spain, Sweden, Switzerland and the United States. More recently, it has occurred in Austria also. This reflected the fact that by 1975 most social security taxes were income-based, whilst many goods and services taxes were imposed as specific rates, and therefore did not rise with the inflation of that period. As between income-based taxes and these taxes there have been few relative changes in the decade to 1986, Italy excepted, though shifts may be expected in future towards indirect taxes because of VAT in states such as Spain, and by later deliberate act.

235. Two other general issues of importance have also surfaced during the period. First is a renewed attention to the undesirability of general high levels of border taxes, through the mechanism of GATT and other agencies. Within the expanded European Communities they are disappearing, and other free trade agreements have potential, if not actual, similar effects. If the aims of the Uruguay Round of GATT are achieved, this will be accelerated – though it must be noted that if the dealine for the end of the planned GATT round passes without agreement, it must be accepted that the short term result may be a reversion towards protectionism.

236. The theory of tax development argues that, as states' economies develop, so their dependence on trade taxes declines – as is clearly so with states such as Spain or Greece. Spanish customs revenues slipped from 3.9% of total taxation in 1975 to 2.8% in 1986, just before the cuts imposed when Spain joined the European Community (which mean of course that Spain can no longer count customs duties as part of its national tax collection exercise). In other European Community states, customs is not part of national taxation (though usually included as such in statistics), but is about 1% of national tax collection.

237. This suggests that the customs duty element of taxation should decline within the OECD and growing economies such as those in South East Asia. Japan illustrates this trend with duties falling from 3.6% of total taxes in 1965, to 1.6% in 1975 and 0.6% in 1986, although they rose slightly in 1987. This is highlighted in the 1989 World Development Report of the World Bank. The Bank's indicators also show that, on the wider category of taxes on international trade and transactions, the average share of revenue derived by a country from this source slipped from 14.1% in 1972 to 10.0% in 1987 in the case of middle income countries, and from 2.3% to 1.2% in the high income economics. India, however, was one economy which went strongly against this trend, increasing its reliance on these taxes from 20% to 28%.

238. The other trend is the rise in the use of wide-based taxes in place of narrower more specific taxes. Above all, we have seen the rise over 30 years of the value added tax. To dismiss this change as easily as Rose did (as quoted at the start of this chapter) overlooks the fact that VAT solved a number of problems with indirect taxes which had bothered tax collectors for centuries. It taxes goods and services alike (most previous taxes did not catch services easily). It is multi-stage, rather than single-stage, it avoids the cascade effect of other sales taxes, and it can (at the cost of border adjustments) be neutral as between imports and domestic production. Because of its very wide base, it is less discriminatory between levels of

production and different products, but at the same time a low rate of tax can raise very significant revenues.

239. Whilst VAT has turned up in some states under disguises or in modified forms (as general sales taxes and goods and services taxes) the spread of comparable taxes to the European Communities' VAT is occurring world-wide. This is partly a direct response by neighbours and trading partners' to the Communities' initiative (as states like Austria, Hungary or Malta evidence), and partly through the adoption of a 'good' idea. Tait has chronicled this very fully in his recent book (published through the IMF), and it would be otiose to cover the same ground here.
Its extent is also charted by Messere and Nørregard in their report for the OECD (Messere and Nørregard, OECD, *Taxing Consumption*, 1989). Their conclusions are:

> It is generally accepted that the most striking development in the tax world over the last two decades has been the spread of VAT. In the mid-sixties VAT did not exist in OECD countries, except in a not fully developed form in Finland and France. By the end of 1988 VAT has been adopted in 18 out of 24 OECD countries and legislation has been passed to bring it into operation in Iceland and Japan in 1989. The Canadian Government also has announced its intention of adopting VAT, so that the only OECD countries uncommitted to VAT are Australia, Switzerland and the United States.

240. They chart the progress of these new taxes in detail, and the extent of the trend is clearly evident, as shown in the accompanying table from that report:

General consumption tax systems in 1967 and 1989

	1 January 1967	1 January 1989	Year VAT introduced
Australia	W	W	No VAT
Austria	C	VAT	1973
Belgium	C	VAT	1971
Canada	M[1]+R[2]	M[1]+R[2]	*
Denmark	W	VAT	1967
Finland	VAT[3]	VAT	1964
France	VAT[4]	VAT	1954
Germany	C	VAT	1968
Greece	M	VAT	1987
Iceland	R	R	1989 (July)
Ireland	W+R	VAT	1972
Italy	C	VAT	1973
Japan	None	None	1989 (April)
Luxembourg	C	VAT	1970
Netherlands	C	VAT	1969
New Zealand	W	VAT	1986
Norway	R	VAT	1970
Portugal	W	VAT	1986
Spain	C	VAT	1986
Sweden	R	VAT	1969
Switzerland	R[5]	R[5]	No VAT
Turkey	None	VAT	1985
United Kingdom	W	VAT	1973
United States	R[6]	R[6]	No VAT

	Number of countries[7]	Number of countries[8]
Single-Stage		
M Manufacture	2	1*
W Wholesale	6	1
R Retail	7	4
Multi-Stage		
C Cascade	7	0
VAT Value added Tax	2	18*
No General Consumption	2	1
	26	25

Notes:
1 At federal level
2 At provincial level
3 Partial only. Full VAT in 1976
4 Partial only. Full VAT in 1968
5 W in certain cases
6 At state and local level only
7 Canada and Ireland counted twice*
8 Canada counted twice*
* (added by DW): Canada's GST was been announced in 1989 and implemented in 1991.
Source: Messere and Nørregard, *Taxing Consumption*.

241. Messere and Norregard offer the following explanation for this process in a summary that deserves extensive quotation:

> A major reason for the choice of VAT was the belief that alone among consumption taxes it had the potential to halt the drastic move in most OECD countries between the early sixties and mid-seventies away from consumption taxes towards income and payroll taxes. VAT duly fulfilled this function. There has been general stability in overall relative reliance on the three major revenue raisers since the mid-seventies, and this has been due to the increase in general rather than selective consumption taxes. However, other reasons are required to explain why this almost universal shift away from consumption taxes occurred and why it was subsequently halted.
>
> During most of the sixties and early seventies the combination of high growth and inflation pushed taxpayers into higher rate tax brackets and at the same time eroded the value of their tax reliefs. This so-called fiscal drag phenomenon enabled income tax revenues to increase without any change in legislation. In addition, with rising standards of living, taxpayers did not protest against, or perhaps did not even notice, the increase in their income tax bills; nor did they object to increases in social security contributions to support their welfare states, especially as these contributions were often perceived as a quasi-insurance payment. Consumption taxes, however, require an increase in rates to bring in more revenue (and in the case of most selective consumption taxes even to raise the same amount of revenue in real terms) and in those heady days most Governments felt no need to take such unpopular measures.
>
> After the first oil shock, with stagflation and falls in real disposable incomes, taxpayers were no longer prepared to pay increasing amounts of income tax and rather demanded reductions or nego-

tiated wage increases in net of tax terms; nor, with increasing levels of unemployment, could payroll taxes remain a buoyant source of revenue. Governments were accordingly forced to turn back to consumption taxation . . .

Finally . . . it is worth emphasising that this trend away from consumption taxes has only been halted, not reversed. A number of Governments have expressed a desire to change the tax mix towards consumption taxes but few have done so in recent years: opposition to perceived distributional consequences and inflationary effects are probably responsible.

242. Since they wrote, attempts have been made by the opposition parties in Japan to rescind the low general comsumption tax newly introduced there, but the Canadian government's report on its proposed goods and services tax have provided a strong defence to the concept. Again, in Canada there was stiff resistance to such a general tax, but in watered-down form it became effective in 1991. At the same time the countries of Eastern Europe were moving towards VAT, with even the government of the USSR adopting a general goods and services retail tax. The latest statistics how a further growth in consumption taxes as a share of total taxation across the OECD in 1987, and suggest a further rise in 1988.

243. Given these changes, VAT-style taxes are unlikely to be lightly abandoned. Whilst interest in the United States has, perhaps, waned in this particular tax reform (though not in the idea of shifting the burden of taxation somewhat from income taxes to goods taxes), the USA is out of line in this respect (as is Switzerland, which refused to adopt one). It is also out of line in the share of taxes collected from goods and services (about 17% of total) compared with most developed states. Japan is also low, but has moved to increase this with its goods and services tax. Switzerland also stands out as having a low and declining goods taxation raised from a turnover tax on goods but not services. It would take something of major significance to shift the European Communities from the VAT entrenched in the Community Treaties, not least because the share of taxation from this and related sources is usually between 25% and 35% of total taxation.

244. This is not to belittle the problems of some states with a VAT-style tax. Federal structures such as the USA, Canada and Switzerland, have major difficulties with it as it does not work well within the forms of federal constitution adopted by them. For example, a major sticking point in Canada was whether the tax should be federal and state, or federal only.

And the Swiss, as has been noted, discarded the idea because of another constitutional issue, the necessity of a plebiscite.

Provincial and local taxation

245. A third shift evident in states generally is a shift from national to local taxes in those states where local taxes are of importance. This shift can arise in several ways. First, as in the United Kingdom, it can occur where there is a shift of expenditure deliberately from central government to local government, without a corresponding shift of central tax revenues. The 'rates' has therefore risen sharply in real terms, itself then causing further concern which has led to the reform of personal taxation through a poll tax, the Community Charge.

246. It is, in this context, worth noting that a major reason for introducing the Community Charge was said – before its introduction – to be that it would control local expenditure by making it more high-profile, and therefore counteract the trend noted. When it was felt, even as the tax was introduced, that it had failed in that aim, other ways of cutting expenditure were sought in order to reduce the level of the tax. Thus what was intended to be the mechanism for reducing expenditure became itself the reason for the reduction by other means and, ironically, a cause for increasing expenditure. It is understood that many were watching this attempt to introduce this new kind of tax and that, had it been perceived as a success, other states might have followed the British lead. It is now difficult to isolate the idea from the context of 'poll tax riots', high political and financial collection costs, and a failed rationale. As with the German withholding tax, one state has suffered long term effects from what may prove a transient attempt to reform, but the world has learnt the lesson.

247. The shift to local taxes may take a different form in federal states, where the central government may curb or cut its public expenditure rather more than local government (as in Canada) or where national programmes of tax reform do not operate on, and have not been reflected by, local taxes (as in the United States). A different effect can occur where local taxation is to some extent parasitic on national taxes (as with the German trade tax and some local Japanese taxes). If the national tax is subjected to a base-broadening and rate lowering exercise, but the rates of local taxes are not lowered as well, the local tax will benefit from the base-broadening noticeably. This has been monitored in Japan, but constitutions may not allow federal authorities to settle local rates of taxation.

248. In the USSR, this tussle between centre and regions has proved particularly sharp, with directly competitive claims for taxation emerging

between the All-Union government and the governments of many of the USSR's 15 republics. Thus in early 1991 we saw the Russian Republic under-cutting the All-Union proposed income tax rates by lower rates of its own.

249. A more general issue also arises. Federal states (Australia, Canada, the CSFR, Germany, Switzerland, the USA, the USSR, Yugoslavia) are, of course, the ones with major local taxes. But they are also the states subject to additional political pressures which have slowed down the process of national tax reform, compared with centralised states. This slowing down has resulted usually in the dilution of proposed reforms at national level if the provinces have competence in the same area of taxation, or if they can affect the revenue-neutrality of reforms. Relative to other states, reform was therefore slow to be realised in, for example, Canada, Germany and Japan, rendering 'before and after' comparisons misleading at present.

250. The largest federal economy, the United States, is instructive. State and local taxation has risen significantly over the last 20 years. In 1965 it formed 32.4% of total taxation, rising to 35.1% in 1975. However, it slipped to 32.4% again in 1980, but rose to 35.0% by 1986. Interestingly, the share of state and local taxes moved sharply upwards in 1987 to 39.2%, against the background of a total rise in revenues of 10.1%. This composite figure hides several underlying and non-coincidental shifts as there is a wide spectrum of local taxes in the United States. A growing share of the main direct taxes shifted to state level. 7.7% of personal income tax was collected at state level in 1965. By 1975 this was 15.0% and by 1986 17.6%, a figure maintained in 1987. The figures were the same for state capital gains taxes on individuals. State corporate income taxes were 7.0% of the total in 1965, 14.0% in 1975 and 24.0% in 1986, though this figure slipped in 1987. State social security contributions rose with national levels. These areas of growth were offset by declining relative levels of tax from property taxation, excises, fiscal monopolies and motor vehicle taxation. Receipts were particularly buoyant, by contrast, from local general sales taxes, and on taxes on specific services. This latter may reflect a 'user charge' approach.

251. The 1986 reforms in the United States involved a major federal-state issue, the deductibility of state taxes against federal taxes. In effect this gives priority to the local taxes over the national taxes. But, because only certain local taxes warranted this deduction, it was assumed that there would be a shift towards deductible taxes rather than other methods of taxing. If there is, it will be a further shift to local taxing. The other effect of the Tax Reform Act was to alter the bases of taxes such as local income

taxes which are defined parasitically by reference to federal law. There is, however, no requirement that the local tax conducts the same base-rate tradeoff that applies nationally, so this may act to further increase local funding.

252. In Canada, there was a similar growth in the provincial share of direct taxes, 29.2% of corporate profits taxes being collected at provincial level in 1986, as compared with 26.7% in 1975 and 23.0% in 1965, the figure rising to over 30% in 1987%. 38% of personal income tax went at provincial level in 1986 compared with 32% (1975) and 24% (1965). On a smaller scale, the same thing happened in Japan with the growth in share of income taxes taken by the prefectural tax and the local inhabitants tax (although the latter yields very limited amounts from corporate taxes). Recent reports from Japan suggesting revision to the property tax may, if taken up, result in that tendency being reinforced.

253. The extent to which this shift has been intended – rather than has 'just' happened – is hard to gauge, as it has been the subject of little comment. It is equally difficult to speculate on the stability or permanence of this shift as in part it reflects the federal budget deficits of states such as the United States, Australia and Canada.

Property taxes

254. A final trend – rather than major shift – relates to the use of wealth and property taxes. The group of taxes taxing wealth or property holding directly or indirectly includes land and habitation taxes, stamp duties on wealth transfers, net wealth taxes, and estates and gift taxes on deaths and lifetime gifts. They may be taken together for convenience, as they are so grouped in the OECD Revenue Statistics. Despite the urgings of some theorists and those seeking to enhance redistribution through the tax system, these taxes have never played a major part in the tax base of any developed state. Over recent years that limited importance has declined in most states, consistent with changed views about the redistributive role of taxation. France has (with some uncertainty) adopted a wealth tax and is to increase its habitation tax, but most states have adopted the opposite approach (France is in an unusual position in having so small an importance attached to its income tax, and therefore so little leeway within that tax to provide for fiscal incentives).

255. In general there has been a firm rejection of major tax-raising through any of these routes at national level. Most particularly, some of the stamp duties, one of the oldest of the kinds of 'modern' taxes, are

being phased out in the European Communities and, by direct competition, elsewhere. Thus, the Communities first imposed a uniform company capital duty on the creation of new share capital of a country, and then advocated its repeal through the Member states. More recently, Member states have indicated their intentions to repeal the stock exchange transfer taxes. Germany, Netherlands and the UK have all announced repeals of these taxes to date. These repeals reflect two effects of the increasing efficiency of international information technology. First, the moves towards paperless transactions of stock make the concept of a 'stamp' obsolete. How do you stamp a computer generated telephone call? Second, we again see tax competition at work, in a market where choice of dealing venue is increasingly price sensitive, and where the main dealing cost is tax.

256. Wealth taxes and gifts taxes are also of limited importance, as evidenced by the 1988 OECD Report, *Taxation of net wealth, capital transfers and capital gains of individuals.* Switzerland was by far the highest user of these taxes (3% of total taxes), all collected at cantonal level. Other traditional users, the Nordic states, have been paring back on their use.

257. Only in three OECD states have all property taxes together recently produced more than 10% of total taxes: Japan, the United Kingdom, and the United States. In the latter, as noted above, property taxes declined sharply in importance between 1965 and 1980 and are largely local taxes. In Japan and in the United Kingdom, the most important of these taxes are the municipal property taxes. From 1990 the United Kingdom has abolished most of its personal municipal property tax, creating instead a poll tax. In 1987 this form of taxation rose as a share of total taxes to over 13%, the highest ratio for over two decades, but that will now be sharply reversed, at least whilst the poll tax survives. It must be commented that the obvious failure of this new tax may lead to a reversion to property taxes. In Japan the level only reached 10% in 1986 for the first time, but rose to over 11% in 1987. Six other OECD states which used to collect 10% or more of total taxes in this way now have not done so since 1975. In the United States it has declined from 15% to 10% since 1965, and only in the United Kingdom, until 1990, has that high share remained relatively steady.

The use of new taxes

258. Sandford and Rose (see chapter 1) counselled against expecting new taxes. Are they right? Broadly, yes. This is, of course, because most forms of tax have been exploited, but there are a few notable exceptions. First is the approach of an expenditure tax. This has been advocated authorita-

tively in a number of countries but has been adopted by none. However, the discussion below notes how features of an expenditure tax which have led advocates to argue its adoption have started to appear in income taxes. Second is a wealth tax, the general rejection of which idea has just been noted. Third is the idea of a cash-flow corporation tax, quite widely discussed but pursued by few. It has attracted some attention in highly inflationary economies, and was recommended for use in the recently adopted Colombian reforms by the leading United States experts who were behind the technical aspects of the reform. The OECD report, *Taxation in developed countries*, notes that when this was discussed in 1987 'it was pointed out that the base for this tax was similar to that for a value added tax.' Though it solved inflation problems, that was then not a major concern.

259. Fourthly, and the most recent arrival, is the pollution tax – taxing a producer to ensure that the producer's sale price reflects external costs (by pollution or the use of non-renewable resources) of a product which otherwise would not be reflected in the producer's production costs. This 'wild' idea of the 1960s is likely to be taken very seriously by 2001, and the OECD's polluter pays principle will quite likely become a stock-in-trade of the tax designer. As yet it has not been adopted comprehensively in any specific state. Even so, the technique has been shown to be effective, as with the Italian tax on plastic bags, which is reported to have cut the number of these bags in use by up to half, and the targetting by a number of states of taxes on cars and car fuel.

260. Of the new taxes that have appeared, VAT is the most significant, and it is difficult to understate the importance of this change. Others – like fringe benefits taxes, social security levies and capital gains taxes – are wider adoption of ideas already accepted. There are few departures from the norm. Perhaps the only one of real note is the United Kingdom's Community Charge, a per capita charge on all residents levied locally. Its swift creation and imposition is a reflection of the highly centralised and government-dominated legislative machinery in Britain, and there are no imitators currently. Its patent failure shows something that no government can afford to ignore, that taxpayers also have to acept these ideas. Perhaps for this reason as for others mentioned above, we should expect few other new ideas.

A summary of shifts

261. The above argues a general shift from direct income-based taxation to other forms of tax, with a rejection of the other possible forms of direct taxation through wealth and wealth transfers, and an aversion to radically

new forms of tax. In the longer term, this means a reversal of the trend evident this century of growing dependence on income taxes. Historically, older states such as France, the Netherlands and Britain relied heavily on indirect taxes, especially customs and excises. Whilst the customs are not available as a revenue source as before, and excises have severe limitations as revenue raisers, the value added tax or general sales tax has been used as the method of attaining a shift, with older taxes being repealed.

262. By contrast, the other major shift – towards social security taxes – reflects the bettering of our societies. Unless we reverse that bettering, or accept the logic of the few states which have merged their social security taxes fully with general taxes, this trend is irreversible in the foreseeable future. This merging, whilst advocated widely by 'theorists', would appear to negate direct tax reforms in a way that makes the merger politically unlikely in most countries. In others the merger could only occur with a major restructuring of the arrangements for social welfare, which again is not likely to happen.

263. There has been a shift into these major forms of tax from the collection of less significant taxes grouped together as property taxes (although varying from transaction duties to net wealth taxes) in all states, and a shift within states with multiple levels of tax collection from the central level to local levels. This has occurred within the collection of direct taxes in some states, accentuating the trend out of national direct taxes.

264. Overall, there is a steady convergence in the kinds of taxes being used by the larger developed states, and the extent to which those kinds of tax are used, and the formal marginal rates at which they are levied. Many of these changes appear spontaneous in the sense that they have not been coordinated or taken in cooperation – or even in direct imitation. However, the cuts in border taxes are clearly the result of combined actions, and the adoption of VAT is due partly to that, and partly to imitation.

Shifts within individual kinds of tax

Radical reformers lightly dismiss 'tinkering' with existing taxes as not being reform, but in practice this is where the main thrust of reform has occurred, with very significant effects on some kinds of activity. In considering the effects of this tinkering, we must pay equal attention to all kinds of income flows : whether earnings from goods, services, employment or capital. More traditionally the first and third of those groups dominated thinking. In current terms, the second, and particularly the fourth, are of growing importance, with the fastest and most uninhibited growth being in flows of capital. The growth in international trade in services, and in capital goods, is evidenced by the 1989 GATT report on international trade. This also evidences a large growth in international trade in capital goods. The international flows of capital have also been highlighted recently, as a side-issue in the 'war' against drugs. What is more, this is where, with '1992' and other similar developments in the major economies, events can move fastest.

Income taxes

266. Changes in income taxes have taken several forms:
shifts between personal income tax and corporate income tax;
measures to reduce the burden and/or the rates of income tax;
and measures to increase the efficiency of corporate taxes.
Each is examined in turn.

Shifts from personal to business taxes

267. This shifting can occur in two ways: a direct policy shift of the burden of tax from the one kind of tax to the other at the macro level, or the reduction of taxation on individual transfers of income from the corporate to individual sectors through imputation, tax credits or other offsetting techniques. There is, however, no clear trend of either kind. Undoubtedly, some states have been able to transfer part of the burden of overall tax on to companies in the 1980s, but this appears as much due to the economic recovery of the period, and the buoyancy of many corporations' profits, as to deliberate policy. The sharply lower profits with which the 1990s have started are likely to see that effect offset significantly. The question of economic double taxation is dealt with below.

Shifts within personal income taxes

268. Within personal income taxes, it has been proposed to 'cut the burden of tax' by:

Reducing overall marginal rates
Reducing the number of rates
Assessing individuals not families
Increasing exemptions for lower incomes
Broadening the tax base
Reducing the number and extent of tax expenditures
Making tax incentives for savings more neutral
Simplifying tax structures
Taxing capital gains as income

269. The simplest of ideas underlies some of these changes: if we broaden the tax base, we can reduce the tax rates whilst not reducing government revenue. If we reduce the tax rates, we reduce the disincentive to work. If we do that, the economy benefits and we collect more tax. We can then cut the tax rates again, and so forth. Add a second aim: let us make the taxes simple. They are far too complex. This is because rates are far too high at the margin, thereby causing high marginal direct and opportunity costs for both compliance and avoidance. If we cut the high rates, taxes will be less unfair at the margin, and we do not therefore need them to be so elaborate. If they are less elaborate they cost us less to collect, and they cost you less to comply with. So down they go again. Finally, a third aim : taxes should be neutral. They should not interfere with what we want to do. They should be fair and tax everyone the same amount regardless of what they do. We shall all be better treated if we get rid of the tax breaks. Add those three aims together (ignoring the fact that they conflict!), and we have the recipe for simple, fair, low taxes.

270. Whilst that may have been the aim, unfortunately or otherwise the world did not work it that way – or has not done so yet. What has been achieved?

(a) *Reducing rates*

271. This has undoubtedly happened, quickly and relatively recently. The OECD report, *Taxation in Developed Countries*, chronicles the changes between 1975 and 1985. Nine of the 22 states had reduced their top rates during that period – but five had increased them. Since then, rates have cascaded down, prompted by the much-heralded cut in the United States (federal rates only) to 15% and 28% from what, 12 years before, had been a 25-rate schedule ranging from 14% to 70%. Serious thought had even been given to a flat-rate tax. Other rate reductions have been shown in the national survey ; the UK from 83% top (98% on investment income), 35% main in 1975 to 40% top, 25% main after the reforms was a forerunner, with a truly staggering *drop* in the top rate of 58%. The latest round shows the Danes cutting their main rates of national income tax from 22% plus 6% plus 12% to 18% plus 8% (the third tax being phased out) over the next three years. With limited exceptions, states have implemented cuts, or announced measures, to bring the top rates down in most cases to 60% or below – and in many states to or below a psychologically important 50%. At the same time the aim appears to be to get the main rates down to about 25%, or lower. The sharpest changes have been in the higher rates, where reforms look dramatic but cost little. But the main rates are also moving down, at considerable cost even for minor changes.

272. Developing states have been following where developed states have led, with countries as diverse as India, Zimbabwe, the Congo, Trinidad, Kenya, Israel, Argentina, Swaziland, Mexico, Korea, Hong Kong, Hungary and Brazil all having announced rate cuts for or in 1989. Malawi, Singapore and Tunisia were some of the states whose rate reductions followed. Not everything goes through (Thailand's proposal was announced, but did not occur), but there is a very clear trend which it will be hard for open economies to counteract (and there must be few candidates for the category of closed economy at present – perhaps Burma being the clearest example, but Albania has ceased so to be). As the integration of the world economy makes it harder for individual states to stand aside (unless in deliberate total isolation), so the trend becomes world-wide.

(b) *increased personal exemptions*

273. Another major shift is towards taking the lower paid out of the income tax net. Again, the United States Tax Reform Act had this as part of its package, with 6 million former taxpayers falling outside the net. The United Kingdom did not see the same reform, the total number of taxpayers (married couples counting as one) being little greater in 1988 than it was in 1968. But in many other states, especially in the last few years, there have been deliberate sharp increases in personal exemptions, zero-rate brackets, credits or other devices to protect low incomes from the income tax.

(c) *increased individual taxation*

274. The move to equal treatment of married (and unmarried couples), which has occurred in countries from Belgium to Zimbabwe, has little to do with the tax reform movement. For example, in Spain individual taxation was imposed by the Supreme Court ruling that family unit taxation was unconstitutional. It is motivated by social and libertarian moves, but has the effect of sharply increasing the numbers of taxpayers, unless counteracted (as in part it will be) by increased personal exemptions.

(d) *streamlined rate schedules*

275. Another part of the United States overall plan was to cut the rates down to two (although it is rightly pointed out that two further rate levels are hidden) from an original two dozen. This again has been echoed by many states. It should presumably simplify administration and understanding by taxpayers of where they stand. It is an equity/efficiency trade-off as are many reforms. Fewer rates means sharper jumps at the end of each rate scale producing increased marginal effects on some, in exchange for greater simplicity for most.

(e) *making capital income more neutral*

276. A series of changes have been aimed at neutralising at least some of

the many distortions in the treatment of passive or capital income. In many countries this has been a mixture of full-rate taxing, sometimes with special higher rates applying to passive income, but offset by various – and sometimes very generous – encouragements to specific investments. The treatment of interest costs, and of receipts from government investments, are particularly in point. About half the OECD states had reliefs or deductions for general interest costs against income in 1985. Most of those reliefs are still in place, although the United States relief is being phased out, and relief has been capped in Spain, and capping is planned in Denmark.

277. Whilst cogent arguments were made for neutrality, this is one area where only a limited amount has been achieved. The French and British are still creating investment incentives, whilst removing others. In part this is now a clear response to international pressure. For example, the freeing within the European Communities of certain unit trusts and mutual funds to trade across frontiers (by the UCITS Directive) promptly led both the British and Irish governments to secure legislation so that their funds were not disadvantaged as compared with the regime applied in Luxembourg. Luxembourg responded aggressively with new tax incentives for venture capital investments. Likewise the French, having failed to secure early Community action against the Luxembourg treatment of interest payments out, announced measures for 1990 to prevent heavy losses of funds when exchange controls are lifted. Belgian reforms to avoid similar losses followed soon after.

278. Belgian measures to exempt savings income on domestic savings, also aimed at the Luxembourg competition, were challenged by the European Commission before the Court, but found not incompatible with European Community rules until a free capital market is established. With this level of activity within the established Community states, little consistency can be expected elsewhere.

(f) *eliminating tax expenditures*

279. The rate-base argument is that by eliminating tax breaks the main rates of tax can be substantially reduced as a revenue-neutral reform. This has not happened. There have been some cuts in less important expenditures, but the main ones : pensions of all kinds, provision of housing for owner-occupation, preferred treatment of benefits in kind, have largely been left alone. Where main rates of income are being cut, this is either being done on a revenue-reducing base (Germany, the United States), or by shifting expenditure from income tax to some other head (taxation of corporations, user charges – as strongly recommended by the World Bank in its 1988 World Development Report, privatisation or, as in Britain and

Denmark, transferring costs from general taxation to social security funding).

280. How far elimination of shelters has occurred seems a matter of opinion even on the United States reforms. Thus, whilst a major protagonist (Joseph Pechman) argued that 'the Act makes a frontal assault on major loopholes and special benefits', Richard Musgrave retorted that 'the Act provides little simplification' and uses 'politically vulnerable provisions to reduce tax rates dramatically.' His standpoint is that of the comprehensive income tax, and he finds that the 1986 Act merely trades one set of distortions for another. Other experts have made similarly strong comments to the present writers. The long-running arguments in 1989 over the proposal to re-introduce a tax deduction in respect of part of capital gains, with the main alternative being to introduce further tax deductions in respect of certain forms of savings, suggests that the serious elimination of tax expenditures in the United States is not high on the current political agenda there. And whilst both in 1989 and 1990 the long-promised changes to the capital gains taxation did not materialise, they were still on the President's agenda in 1991.

281. More generally, the extent of scope for base-rate tradeoffs may be exaggerated under some systems, as the Oort Commission illustrated. This is a problem where the extent of tax expenditures varies markedly from one country to another. It is therefore relatively easier for some states to finance tax cuts by base-broadening than it is for others.

282. Further, the true elimination of tax expenditures runs contrary to the other trends already noted, that is, to protect the lower income recipients from income tax by higher exemptions rather than, as some would see, much lower rates applied to all income.

283. Deductions against employment income, and privileged treatment of employees and those with replacement incomes are also in point. The United States and Britain extended their tax bases by making certain social security receipts, previously exempt from tax, now subject to tax, but neither convincingly tackled benefits in kind. The 'cafeteria' approach to remuneration is still effective in the United States and, whilst there are some special measures against many benefits in kind in the UK, they are still tax preferred (for example, being exempt from social security tax). The major expense of most employees - the cost of purchasing a house – still retains generous tax relief in just about all OECD countries, and attempts to remove this relief seem politically impossible, even if the OECD's own staff fell it desirable (as was suggested in the 1989 report by the OECD for the UK).

284. Although a number of states now implementing reforms (the Netherlands, Denmark, Germany) do seem intent on genuine simplification and offsetting of rates against bases, the measures so far may best be described, along the lines of Musgrave's comments, as decisions to reduce income tax rates funded by means which include the elimination of some tax expenditures, but not anything too politically sensitive. This is far short of the ideals of the economists who produced Treasury I and other proposals, although it is probably very sound national politics.

(g) *treating capital gains as income*

285. In one area, more solid progress has been suggested. This is in the treatment of capital gains as income. But has it occurred? Again, this was tackled by the 1986 Tax Reform Act. 1989 saw the arrival on the floor of the House of a proposal to re-introduce a tax 'break' for most forms of capital gains. At one time it appeared that the President had secured a majority in Congress to support his administration's proposals to reintroduce a 30% deduction before tax in the value of major categories of gains. Whilst this would have left the effective tax on gains somewhat higher than it was prior to earlier US reforms, it would have reintroduced a major differentiation within the so-called comprehensive tax base of the US federal income tax. Britain and France have both tightened their treatments of capital gains, as has Finland and, in a limited way, the Netherlands. More generally the Netherlands and New Zealand, both countries without capital gains tax, are still talking about introducing one, although Italy (another OECD state not taxing capital gains) is planning to introduce a limited capital gains tax. Belgium's action was first confined only to closing a loophole in the Belguim-Sweden double tax agreement allowing Swedish taxpayers to sidestep the Swedish tax. What is clear is that, generally, the idea that income and capital gains are different entities is disappearing as an approach to tax design. At the same time, the rates at which these taxes apply leaves capital gains much more highly taxed in some states than others.

(h) *anti-avoidance measures*

286. Finally, dramatic extensions to the tax base can occur through anti-avoidance measures, and this effect has occurred in a number of states. It is perhaps more important in the business tax field, and is noted there.

Shifts within corporate income taxes

287. The pattern of shifts is similar to that for individual income tax except that, prior to reform, the general rates of tax were noticeably higher than main rates of individual income tax, and the importance of

relevant tax expenditures was greater. The reforms have therefore had more room for progress, and this has been achieved.

(a) *rate reductions*

288. Corporate tax rates were not usually imposed on complicated rate schedules, but on main basic rates. Those rates were often at 50% or above, but have shifted markedly downwards and are converging towards a common rate of about 34% – 39%. 35% was in 1989 (reducing to 33% in 1991) the United Kingdom rate and is the 'upper' profits rate in the Netherlands, and the Danish target. The United States' rate is 34% as is Luxembourg's, with states such as Singapore a little below. Australia's rate has dropped to 39%, as has the undistributed rate for France, with Japan aiming at 37.5% and the German split rate producing 36%. The cuts are an unfinished process and the downward convergence may be predicted to continue, although there are exceptions. New Zealand was forced to put a cut to 28% for resident corporations and 33% for non-residents into reverse by a 5% hike in 1989 (perhaps it realised it had overshot), and Ecuador's cuts were reversed in 1988. Other states have stalled more permanent cuts by temporary surcharges, as in Brazil where the cut in the main rate from 35% to 30% was without prejudice to surcharges.

289. Why 34% to 39%? The US rate reform was based, according to one of its designers (McClure), on the thought that the corporation tax should be a little, but not too much, above the rate (28%) for higher income earners under the individual tax. That basis does not apply in Britain, where the 35% rate is below the upper income tax rate. Perhaps it is a nice number at round about one-third of income. What does seem to have happened is that the USA and UK set a target which an aggressive competitor such as the Netherlands was prepared to meet and others such as France and Germany respect, with the result that everyone else took note.

290. There would seem to be a clear case of 'me too' about these rate cuts as other countries, such as Ireland, which find cuts hard to finance, still attempt to push their rates towards the target range (their rate will be down to 43%). International competition would seem the likely cause of the particular pattern of changes emerging, although the broader justification of lower rates producing less distortion is a sound rationale. One latecomer to the arena of change, Canada, was most forthcoming in noting the pressures on it for rate reduction especially in the corporate sector, because of international comparisons.

291. Nonetheless, the comparability of rates is superficially much clearer than is the picture if the effective rates of tax on retained and distributed

profits is noted. Within any one economy this varies widely depending on the nature of the business. Between states the variations are wider still because of different methods of defining taxable profits, including varying forms of tax expenditure, and because of the differing arrangements to grant credit for the underlying tax paid on profits when dividends are brought into charge.

(b) *base broadening*

292. It is entirely plausible, as American commentators argued for the US reforms, that base broadening for the corporation tax was designed to finance predetermined rate cuts, rather than the original approach of identifying expendible tax expenditures and base extensions and using those to reduce the rates as far as they would. If so, that would explain the patchy approach to the reform of tax breaks. There are still major differences between the ways companies in different developed states calculate profits for corporate tax purposes. Initiatives by the European Community to find a common base for taxing businesses in the Community have so far only served to emphasise the major differences between the attempted objectivity of the British system and the accounts-based approach of the Germans.

293. During much of the period under review strong conflicts occurred over one variant in calculating profits, the unitary tax. Whilst economist reformers argue this wide tax base as an appropriate approach for both state and national tax authorities, its firm rejection by Japan, the European Community, the United States federal authorities and others makes an interestingly sharp response to the idea, at least in its Californian form. The approach was one which recognised one of the key problems of current taxation of multi-nationals' business profits – the inability to locate within one state the proper share of profits due to that state by reference to declared revenues alone. It has also been urged by some as the answer to the problems of taxing corporations within the European Community. But both governments and the multinationals gave the idea short shrift.

294. If that approach – namely a carve-up of the corporation's total profits on a world-wide basis – is not a practical option, the alternatives must be in rationalising the calculation of profits. Some states have made significant progress in eliminating some tax expenditures from the tax base (by reducing inventory reliefs, and reducing the tax incentives to capital investment or specific kinds of job creation) with a direct trade-off in rate reduction. The United Kingdom undoubtedly led the way in that respect, and was able to do so partly at the cost of inflation reliefs which – temporarily – did not matter. But no attempt has been made to tackle all

expenditures in this way. There has been a broad move on certain topics – entertainment charges for example are now generally not deductible – but others – corporate pension schemes – have not been touched.

295. If the tax remains a charge on net profits, broad scope for deductions and for arguments over the capital-income divide remain. Avoiding this could be achieved through cash-flow taxes (which have been little discussed) or through a charge on gross, rather than net, profits. But this is what we have in the value added tax. To the extent that there is a shift out of direct taxes to value added taxes, it is a shift away from the 'net' profit concept to a charge on the full profits allowing deductions only for capital and revenue overheads as incurred but ignoring payroll costs and (in the present form of VAT) finance charges.

296. In eliminating, for example, relief for capital expenditure so as to expand the tax base, allowance is made for payroll costs but not capital invested. Clearly these differing approaches can have profoundly different impacts on different kinds of business in terms of effective tax rates. One view of recent reforms is that it has shifted the heavier burdens from some kinds of commerce to others, without introducing any real neutrality. What was bad news to leasing businesses in Britain (but not Ireland) was good for those with highly taxed profits, who gained from the rate reductions without losing major allowances. This suggests that the base-rate reforms for corporate taxes has no inherent logic within a 'net' profit context, as against the rationale for personal taxes where it is quite possible to eliminate almost all tax allowances, at least in theory. To that statement one major qualification is needed, the treatment of tax shelters.

(c) *eliminating tax shelters*

297. A major thrust of the United States reform was to eliminate shelters from tax. In the endeavour, it was pursuing a consistent federal drive to deal with avoidance, both internal and jurisdictional (that is, by moving taxable finance outside the tax jurisdiction). The change was that there was seen to be a direct trade-off for those taxpayers not avoiding, and also a marginal cut in the benefits of avoiding. Was this a world-wide trend?

298. At the level of internal avoidance there are profound differences in systems. The Anglo-American common law world has an approach to tax legislation akin to crime laws. They can only be applied when, without doubt, they reach the particular facts. Change the facts, and the crime laws do not apply. Avoidance is thus part of the permissible approach (indeed, of course, you are *meant* to avoid the crime laws). Similarly, with tax laws avoidance is fully acceptable.

299. Contrast the approach of civil law states, and by analogy states such as Russia. There the spirit of the law is much more important. The spirit of the law, especially broadly written laws like the Code Napoleon, is of the essence. It is not permissible to ignore it – it is an 'abus de droit'. Through a combination of statutory and judicial bars, most civil-law states block the sort of avoidance widely practiced in Britain. Again, the absence of elaborate property ownership laws, such as the discretionary trust, in civil law systems also reduce the chances of avoidance. In other countries again, such as Japan, taxpayer compliance is higher and opportunities to avoid will not be pursued to the same extent, thus allowing the government to rely more on consensus.

2000. 'System avoidance', as it might be called in Britain, has been tackled by the courts in the United States for many years. In 1981 it was tackled in Britain in an unlikely piece of tax reform, through the famous judgment of our House of Lords in *Ramsay* v *IRC*. This imported a weak form of the United States doctrine into United Kingdom tax law. *Ramsay* was seized upon by tax administrations in several other countries, and led to important decisions in the courts of Canada, Ireland, India and New Zealand. It also reinvigorated the consideration of statutory bars against system avoidance (particularly as a reaction to the decisions of the courts in Canada and Ireland against judicial anti-avoidance laws). As a result, most common-law states now have an anti-systems-avoidance approach akin to that of civil-law states.

2001. Neither approach stops other kinds of avoidance, such as the payment of earnings in kind rather than cash. This is less a systems problem than a problem of definition within an individual tax code. Fringe benefits have been tackled by several OECD states in recent years, as an OECD study and report, *Taxing Fringe Benefits*, recently showed. The Australian and New Zealand Fringe Benefits Taxes have already been mentioned. But here, as elsewhere, removal of tax cxpenditures has been partial. Greece, which does not tackle non-system avoidance, does not attempt to deal with it. Britain deals with it in part, as does Ireland, under one income tax but not the other (social security tax). The United States federal laws touch it but lightly, ignoring issues such as medical expenses and insurance. There is, however, no uniformity, and wide statements oversimplify. For example, Germany and the Netherlands both have wide laws catching benefits in kind, but allow deductions for the cost of travelling to work. Britain has narrower laws, but does not allow travel deductions.
The 'benefit' of free season tickets (now stopped) and 'cheap' loans to buy season tickets appears as tolerated avoidance in Britain, but as a proper tax allowance in other Community states.

2002. Jurisdictional avoidance relates directly to problems of double taxation, and is dealt with in part II of this report. It will there be noted that there has been significant pressure in developed states to expand the tax base by extending the definition of what is within a state's taxes, and also redefining transactions and arrangements partly internal and partly overseas.

2003. In summary, determined attempts have been made by many states to tackle some kinds of avoidance – particularly, elaborate avoidance schemes in those states where this was possible. However, this does not seem to be a part of any particular 'reform' package. Certainly, the judges in the British courts would not see it as such. Rather, it is part of a long term process in fully developed countries where evasion is controlled to the point that avoidance becomes an important activity – a stage which Spain and Italy have reached in the period under review, but others like India have yet to confront.

(d) *treatment of dividends*

2004. The legal independence of companies from their shareholders, and of subsidiary companies from their parent companies, is the normal rule applied in tax law. Different rules are applied to the recognition of the economic reality of a corporate group (both to assist taxpayers and to counter avoidance), although (subject to double taxation agreements) barriers are often drawn within groups that operate in more than one tax jurisdiction. Although this difference can be most important, the fundamental issue is how generally the relationship between company and shareholder is regarded.

2005. There have long been major differences between states about whether they should use the so-called classical system and treat the dividend paid to a shareholder as unrelated to the profits earned by the dividend-payer (and therefore already taxed), or whether so offsetting should be provided to recognise the economic double taxation of the classical system. There are, of course, several differing methods of relieving the double tax.
They have differing effects when double tax relief is applied, as explored below. Has this issue of double tax been part of the reform movement?

2006. There has been no change in their respective rules by either of the prime movers for reform, the United States and the UK, both firmly committed to radically differing systems. Other states have made major changes. Australia adopted a full imputation system in 1987, but by contrast Canada that year increased the tax it imposed on intercompany dividends that were not distributed by the recipient. However, Canada did introduce for the first time measures recognising the existence of groups. France and Luxembourg both extended the situations in which they would grant participation exemption to a shareholder on dividends on its shareholding, whilst the Netherlands took steps described as having 'serious consequences' against Dutch companies with overseas subsidiaries to restrict their participation exemption from dividend withholding. Germany moved to simplify its imputation system, but changed its split rates of tax on distributed and undistributed profits so as to require, in its view, a renegotiation of many double tax agreements.

2007. For many years, international discussion of the problem achieved little. Earlier moves by the European Community Commission (which had proposed a common imputation system throughout the Community) made no progress for many years, and were formally withdrawn in 1990. The 1987 French/OECD seminar concluded only that 'There is room for attention here by the OECD' ,and for more research and fact-finding.

Shifts within value added and similar taxes

2008. Although the arrival of VAT is itself fairly new, the tax is already subject to rate-base adjustments. There is widening of the tax base within the European Communities, as exemptions and zero-rates are eroded by agreed actions, by judgments of the European Court and by national initiatives, and as the Commission takes repeated action against national failures to implement the requirements of Community law. Under Commission pressure or Court action the use of zero-rating has been restricted noticeably. The lowest rates of tax have been raised. At the same time the highest rates (luxury rates in France and Ireland for example) have been cut back and the number of different levels of tax have been reduced, normally not now exceeding three.

2009. The main rates, used for increasing categories of supplies, are converging on the 15% to 20% bracket. Such actions are openly associated with the move to a Single Market in 1993. With several states as, or wishing to be, candidates for membership of the European Community, the convergence of EFTA initiatives with those of the European Community, and the adoption by Hungary and Poland of western European approaches to taxation a consistent continent-wide tax framework is slowly but steadily emerging.

2010. On a wider front, new entrants to the VAT/GST field have watched and learned from earlier states, as Canada, the latest to adopt its new GST, has borrowed from the European Community (particularly Britain) and New Zealand. Whilst there has been considerable divergence on politically sensitive issues such as taxing food, the logic of the tax – to provide a very wide base in taxing most ordinary commercial supplies of goods and services at a flat rate – is slowly spreading.

Chapter 3

A review of national reforms

And pluck till time and times are done
The silver apples of the moon
The golden apples of the sun
W B Yeats, Song of the
Wandering Aengus

300. Having noted various patterns and kinds of reform, in this chapter we attempt to draw some aspects of change together. In doing so, it is emphasised that it is no part of this work to advocate any particular reform, or indeed any at all. It is merely observing what has happened, what is said to be happening, and reflecting on what may or may not happen. It was argued at length in the previous chapter that reform was inherently an unlikely activity in the tax field, but that nonetheless it was clear that many states felt obliged to take some part (or at least to appear to be taking some part) in the movement of reform. Several aspects of that reform appear to have made changes to tax systems which are unlikely to recede in foreseeable conditions:

1) Fiscal barriers to imports and exports are on the wane in both the developed and developing worlds. Despite the dramatic growth in the total value of international trade and transactions, the temptation to use it as a base for taxation is being resisted. Such duties as appear in most states are specific and protective and are more in the nature of a penalty than a levy. We explore the problems of this area later, but we argue that the trend is, in the short term, not going to be reversed.

2) Among the developed and upper-middle income developing states, specific social security taxes will, with very few exceptions, become more significant taxes. Social welfare costs will steadily grow in the share of total tax expenditure they absorb on all likely predictions, because of the aging of populations. However, it seems politically unlikely in either Europe or North America that many states will in the short term be attracted to combining their specific social security taxes with more general taxation.

3) The 'user charge' element of taxation will increase. There are several reasons for this. One clear trend has been to increase 'charges' to reduce taxation – although in many analyses the so-called charges may be better regarded as taxes. Some states do so classify them (see the list of specific taxes in Denmark) where others will not do so (as in the United Kingdom). We have noted the increase in local taxation, where the 'user charge' approach is clearer, particularly where taxes are levied by local municipalities for immediate local expenditure. Finally, any serious espousal of anti-pollution and pro-environmental policies are quite probably going to include various specifically targeted tax provisions on the polluter-pays principle advocated strongly by the OECD.

4) On current trends, highly developed states will continue to play down the role of direct profits taxes in tax systems , particularly personal income tax; less developed states will continue to rely on it more heavily, but perhaps more often in presumptive or simplified forms. Marginal rates of tax will fit into the new patterns noted in the last chapter, but there will be no major shift towards comprehensive income taxation. Changes in income taxation will rely on other taxes – or inflation taxation – to fund their needs.

5) General sales taxes and turnover taxes will provide a temptingly easy and large share of taxation in most non-federal states. Unless the European Commission succeeds in persuading the member states of the need to change to an origin based tax from its present destination-based approach, it is likely to evolve in an import-neutral mode, with exporting states exempting goods and importing states charging them.

6) Avoidance activity will continue to grow, nationally and internationally. This will be encouraged by the growth in the number of low-tax states offering special tax systems of interest to those based elsewhere. Anti-avoidance activity will also rise, and we explore the international aspects of that below. This will increase the pressure to move to tax bases and methods that are less susceptible to avoidance.

7) Particularly because of the reasons in 2) above, attempts by advanced states to cut total taxation – at least in a realistically wide sense of the meaning of the term, rather than any narrower definitions excluding 'charges' for internal domestic political reasons – seem likely, on most economists' predictions, to be of limited success. Future changes will, at best, have to be revenue neutral in most major states.

8) The changes that have occurred and will occur will be interactive and self-reinforcing. By that we mean that any plateau of rates or consensus

about tax forms will be subject not just to internal political inertia, but to external restraint because of the relative costs to most economies of stepping out of line with prevailing approaches to taxation.

Stability of the changes

301. It is widely said that recent tax reform measures have two areas of weakness in their potential stability : inflation and budget deficits. The reform measures of the last decade followed a period of relatively high inflation and came at a time when inflation was, by recent standards, much lower in the most heavily developed states (with one or two even recording negative inflation rates). Without being sidetracked into discussions beyond the scope of this work, it may be noted that inflation could be said both to have been a cause of the need for reform, and, with its cyclical changes, to have provided a means for that reform.

302. The cause was the effect of fiscal drag, that is, the automatic effects of inflation upon a tax structure. In most tax systems, until recently, little account was taken of inflation in a direct sense. The effects were, rather, on the distortions that inflation caused to the relative effectiveness of existing tax bases. Taxes such as customs duties and many excises, which are specific duties levied at set levels on quantities rather than values of goods and services, decrease sharply unless conscious decisions are made to raise them. However, raising indirect taxes will of itself raise prices, and therefore cause a further measure of inflation of a kind which is attributable directly to government.

303. Direct taxation, the traditional analysis runs, is directly related to income levels, and is therefore dragged up in cash terms with the cash gains in profits. There is therefore a steady shift towards the direct taxes from the indirect taxes. That has been well recognised politically for some years. One consequence was the building-in to direct tax provisions of inventory reliefs and other means of preventing the taxation of inventory profits and of unduly deterring capital investment.

304. When the need to remove tax expenditures to finance rate reductions became important, those reliefs were, in several Western states, of limited importance. The inflation rate in the UK had, for example, shrunk from 25% to 3% in a few years (though it has since risen back into double figures). Imposing an inflation tax at the level of 3% to 5% on stock and investment was politically quite easy if the offset was a reduced tax rate. Further, it had the benefit of downgrading, with instant effect, the values of all past unclaimed tax allowances of these kinds as the rate reduced.

Will those removals and reductions survive as inflation again rises? Or will the pressures of higher inflation, if it does appear as a general feature of developed economies, force the reintroduction of special reliefs?

305. The same effects will be evidenced in personal income taxes if inflation increases. The more recent trends have been to remove sizeable numbers of lower-earner taxpayers from the coverage of the personal direct taxes. This has been linked with, and has assisted, the introduction in several states of individual taxation rather than family taxation. Inflation at any significant level will quickly reverse such a trend and will, as in the past, provide a ready source of extra taxation even if the allowances are supposed to be adjusted by reference to inflation.

306. Another aspect of inflation is the attractiveness of proportional taxes. The earlier part of the reform period saw states having to raise significant extra social security funds. They did so in a number of countries by converting schemes based on flat-rate premiums on to an income-based approach. These therefore creep upwards with the earnings on which they are based. VAT is also a 'creeping' tax in that sense. What is more, unless action is taken to increase the rate at which VAT is levied, the upward increase in VAT collected remains hidden in a way that other specific consumption taxes do not.

307. Future inflation will therefore have a wider effect on tax systems such as those of Western European states than in the past, with the shift towards income and company taxes not being so clear.

308. The other weakness in the pattern of reform is that changes have occurred at a time when states managed to curb total expenditure, and hold the total share of taxes as part of GDP at a roughly level proportion. Even so, the level is creeping slowly up. The OECD figures for a three-year rolling average show that the unweighted average increase from the period 1983-85 to 1985-87 was from 37.0% of GDP to 38.1% of GDP. In only two countries was there a decrease over this period : Luxembourg saw a decrease of 0.5%, caused by a very sharp increase in 1983 abating in the following years (but with a noticeable increase in 1987), and Portugal, where the diminution is 0.1%, but the provision at figures for 1988 suggest a recent sharp increase in total taxes.

309. This slow creep still leaves the United States and several other major economies in deficit, or with major sectors or aspects of the economy (specifically social security funding) in potentially exposed positions. Revenue-losing reforms cannot be afforded. They must at best be revenue-neutral, and then on the basis that some other area of the tax sys-

tem will show an offsetting increase. The Australasian states have, for example, been embarrassed by excessive reductions. The 1987 World Bank figures show a total deficit of all reporting economies of 4.8% of GNP, with the figure for the high-income economies at a deficit of 4.3%. Put another way, to emphasise the shortfall, total central government revenues of the high-income states was in 1987 only 85% of total central government expenditure.

310. Which taxes will be increased? One answer might be a multiplicity of charges and minor taxes. This appears in the United States where the means of funding the capital gains cut proposed by the incoming Bush administration ranged from the 3% charge on long distance telephone calls to an environmentally friendly tax on substances which attack the ozone layer (and perhaps the first of the 'green' taxes predicted above). Similar tactics followed the climb-down in mid-1990 from the 'no new taxes' promise. But the trend is away from that, because of administrative simplicity. Another may be to use the moral arguments available to increase taxes on 'undesirable' goods (and services?) – but if people do give up smoking, the long-term public expenditure rises, and public revenue slippage, will be important.

311. The logic of political expediency would suggest four target areas for increases: social security taxes, presented as non-tax increases or as 'ear-marked' taxes somehow not meeting 'general' government expenditure; value added taxes or general sales taxes – by whittling away exemptions and lower rates as much as by increasing main rates; personal (but not corporate) direct taxes, by allowing fiscal drag to creep back in again, and by removing some of the more expensive tax expenditures (if not outright, by allowing them to waste away); and generally by more aggressive anti-avoidance and anti-evasion activity, especially with regard to tax losses to activities outside the tax jurisdiction.

Tax havens

312. The last of these trends is one to which we must also pay some attention. Alongside the reforms on which we have been concentrating have been another set of reforms : those of states turning themselves into low-tax territories for some purpose or other.

313. One important list of states tends to get left out of sets of statistics. These are the states and territories (55 in total in 1989) with populations measured in thousands rather than millions. The biggest of them – Luxembourg for example – do appear, but others are minute. Nonetheless they have become masters at selling themselves and their services for those wishing to avoid tax, and any analysis of tax trends must note this.

314. The point is well-made by the Introduction of the fifth edition of Grundy's Tax Havens (1987). It notes that the first edition in 1969 covered 14 territories. By 1983 this had grown to 19, due to the 'huge growth of the offshore industry in the last 20 years'. For the 1987 edition there are 24 entries 'and even then I had to leave out Andorra, Bahrain, Costa Rica, Djibouti, Grenada, Montserrat, Nevis, St Vincent, Seychelles, Singapore, South Africa, Swaziland, and the US Virgin Islands' – and even then he left out American Samoa, Aruba, Belize . . . and the states, like Malta, considering how best they can get involved in the area. The full list is perhaps best seen by looking at those published by the revenue authorities of the major states in association with the anti-avoidance activities – or by looking at the list of states with small populations and territories.

315. The trends here have been as much shaped by the leaders in the market as have the reforms amongst the most developed states. At the core of the system provided by these leaders is the ability, within the current international tax system, and seemingly tolerated by the larger states, to provide a low-tax or no-tax regime for businesses centred there which is acceptable for international double tax purposes. One undoubted trend in recent years is that this benevolent acceptance of havens has become too expensive and widely used to be allowed to continue unabated. This has resulted in attempts to ensure that tax is claimed in the developed states in respect of activities based in the havens. This has coincided, as we note below, with other pressures on tax havens.

Getting others to pay

316. The trend against tax havens can be presented as part of a broader trend evidence in more recent years, and which may grow. This is the move towards imposing upon others as much as one can of the national tax burden. An aggressive view of what is within the tax jurisdiction of a state is, perhaps, to be expected for two separate reasons at the present time: the continuing search for new sources of revenue to alleviate the budget deficit whilst not increasing tax rates, and the growing ease with which national tax jurisdictions can, in a physical sense, be avoided.

317. As an American commentator (Ross) noted in 1988:

> Tax collectors the world round are becoming more aggressive in imposing taxes on foreign persons. Thus while the United States may be leading the way, it is not alone . . .
>
> A closely related issue is whether the U.S. developments will lead to increased cooperation internationally or will be counterproduc-

tive from that standpoint. The United States took many actions which are directly inconsistent with tax treaty obligations and others which suggest a unilateral nationalistic approach rather that an internationally cooperative approach to international tax issues. Whether other countries in response to this will also seek to take unilateral action or whether they will renew their efforts to try to establish international cooperation remains to be seen. Certainly on this score the United States should make every effort to cooperate internationally to help other nations adjust to its changes. Whether this will happen remains to be seen.

318. As recent United States discussions indicate, this search for extra revenues from the edges of a state's tax jurisdiction is legislative as well as administrative, and it is one in which the OECD has been actively involved for some time. But it presents a paradox, or perhaps a contradiction. We noted, as the first trend summarised in this chapter, the wasting away of customs duties and most forms of taxation on international trade. We end the chapter by noting two trends which appear directly to contradict this. What is clear is that the international implications of national changes are likely to be operating at several levels.

319. The problems are better seen by another United States commentator (Summers in 1988), who offers a clearer view of the direction the world's most important tax system will take:

> Until recently, international taxation has been an arcane subspecialty among American tax lawyers, and international considerations have rarely influenced the thrust of tax reform. Instead, tax rules have been crafted in consultation with domestic interests; tax incentives have been instituted to spur American individuals and companies to work toward perceived national goals; and the overall level of tax collections has been determined on the basis of American business conditions. Such a provincial approach to tax policy may have been appropriate in an earlier era, but the increasing economic integration of the world requires a more global approach to tax policy. The emphasis in recent American tax reform debates on competitiveness is only a precursor to a time in which international considerations will play a pervasive role in shaping tax policies.
>
> If nations pursue tax policies without regard to international objectives, the result will inevitably be economic conflict. Competition among nations will make it difficult to effectively tax multinational companies, and inconsistent policies toward saving and investment will give rise to disruptive trade imbalances.

320. Bird makes the same point in a broader way the same year:

> We have all become aware that we live in an increasingly integrated world. Politically, however, the sovereignty of nations remains paramount. New nations are understandably nervous about again subordinating themselves to influences from beyond their borders. Old nations are equally reluctant to give up their right to shape their own destiny. International policy coordination is sporadic, loosely if at all institutionalized, subject to substantial national variation, and at best partially effective in achieving its supposed objectives.
>
> Nevertheless, the international dimension of economic policy has become increasingly important. Monetary interdependence, trade imbalances, international capital flows, direct foreign investment, and other transborder linkages trouble the minds and influence the actions of policy-makers in all countries, large or small, rich or poor.
>
> Circumstances will in any case force countries gradually to approximate their tax rules (if not necessarily rates) in order to achieve more acceptable policy outcomes. The question is whether by working together the results will be better for all concerned than by leaving the outcome entirely up to the market.

321. Implicit in the final question is the acceptance that states are not working together in the design of their national tax systems (and, indeed, we have quoted Bird above as advising developing states not to do so). Do they, and can they, work together in dealing with international double taxation and international aspects of tax avoidance and evasion? That we consider next. Before we do, it is worth reviewing the trends shaping such considerations – which can best be done, perhaps, by shaping the questions the answers to which, at any point in time, indicate the stage at which progress has been made.

A summary of trends

322. The political, economic and fiscal climates have all conduced to promote tax reform high on the political agenda of many states. This reform has resulted in a number of changes to tax systems. Whilst these changes have been more limited than the proposals put forward in most states, and have only partially met the expectations of those proposing reforms, they are significant. How much longer will the process continue? Are we now seeing a downward spiral in tax systems, or merely a catching up exercise

by the laggards? Is the political momentum for reforms running out, or will the sensitivity of tax issues remain a continuing stimulus to reform ? Already by 1990 the assumptions of many were that the 90s will see the end of the reforms and the renewal of the upward creep of tax takes.

323. Inevitably, the question arises as to how stable and long term these reforms are. In particular, the reforms were pushed through in a period of low inflation. What will happen as inflation increases noticeably? Will states be able to maintain the reduced levels of relief on inventory and indexing if inflation gains momentum? The other instability is the underlying fiscal deficits of most economies. How will tax reforms be handled if these fiscal deficits get beyond acceptable levels? Given that the long-term costs of government of most developed states will not decrease, where will the extra tax come from?

324. Whilst the reforms are motivated partly by internal factors, they have also undoubtedly been influenced by external competition. It may be assumed that this pressure on individual economies will grow. Should states talk more actively about parallel reforms (aside from the European Communities) or should they let their systems compete? If they do let their systems compete, how do they deal with tax havens and international avoidance?

325. One major change lies in the social security cost burdens on states. Will this be met by increasing social security taxes? Or will the burden fall on general taxes? Will the growing awareness that tax is paying for social security cause any changes in general tax systems, such as merging general and social security payroll and earnings taxes?

326. Is the trend towards a growing share of revenue being collected at provincial and local level a deliberate one? Is it one that will continue?

327. Will there be growth in the replacement of taxes with user charges? How, in the borderline areas between taxes and user charges, is the difference defined? Does it matter?

328. The extent to which tax bases for personal tax have been broadened is limited, and counteracted by the growth of exemptions for the poor. Will this continue, or will inflation erode these allowances? Will serious attempts be made to introduce a comprehensive income tax, or is the US measure to re-introduce a capital gains tax reduction the first sign of general backsliding? Has the process of base-broadening already achieved a politically optimum level.

329. Tax reform for personal taxes has taken the form of reduction in the main and higher rates of tax. Are these reforms likely to be reversed? Higher rates in several states have fallen to 50% or below. Will this trend continue? Is anything gained by the reduction in the numbers of rates of tax?

330. The corporate main tax rate has come down to 34% to 39% in major states. Will this become a universal rate? If so, will it force states steadily to extend their tax bases, or to shift taxation on to other taxes? Can states individually now afford to increase their tax rates markedly unless others do? Will there be any serious attempt to reach an international consensus on the resolution of the problem of economic double taxation of corporate profits/dividends?

331. Little systematic has emerged from the move towards rationalising the taxation of capital income on savings, or the capital gains realised on assets, although several states are still examining these questions. Should more have been expected here? Is more likely to occur?

332. Property and wealth taxes are seldom a popular source of income, and they have decreased in importance in most developed states. Is this, and are they, significant?

333. Aside from the Community Charge and the Fringe Benefits Tax, there have been no new taxes of note on direct income. In particular, arguments for cash-flow taxes and expenditure taxes have been ignored. Should that be so?

334. Customs duties form a declining source of revenue. Should it be recognised that revenue duties other than protective duties are now outdated for developed economies?

335. Value added tax has replaced other general forms of taxation on goods and services. This appears unlikely to be reversed in the near future. Should the tax remain in the form of a multi-stage consumer tax on the destination principle? Is there a 'natural' rate for VAT, and are national rates converging towards 15% to 20%?

336. Specific taxes on goods and services have always been a ready way of dealing with particular problems for economies short of revenue sources. Will international factors discourage this?

337. Overall, developed tax systems are converging towards a selected few kinds of taxes to raise most of their revenues, and the rates of those taxes are also converging. Will this put smaller economies – or in due

course *all* economies – into a form such that they are prevented by competitive pressures from wide divergence. If so, what effect will that have on the government process?

338. The questions that follow the logic of that approach go to the heart of the taxing process and of the nature of the sovereign independent state as it has evolved in recent times, and indeed to the nature of taxation itself as the means by which governments finance those activities they choose to finance and redistribute between their peoples the wealth of nations.

Chapter 4

International tax reform?

Oui, cela était autrefois ainsi, mais nous avons changé tout cela
Molière, Le Medécin malgré lui

400. 1977 saw the conclusion of the second version of the OECD Model Double Taxation Convention, revised after 14 years' experience of the 1963 draft. Would a new revision be appropriate in 1991 after another 14 years? Although some have suggested a new revision is appropriate, it is understood that there will be no new convention in the near future, but rather that the OECD is working to consolidate its discussions since 1977 with a view to supplementing rather than replacing the 1977 model.

401. This is not to say that change is not occurring. There is a constant refinement and clarification of positions by all the states involved. For example, the extent of reservations made by states to the commentaries on the 1977 model have, over time and with experience, been clarified and spelt out to actual and potential treaty partners. The forms of particular clauses have been subject to interpretation and consideration, which itself has reflected into the forms of wording used in actual treaties. Again, much attention has been paid to strengthening the terms in individual treaties designed to deal with problems of avoidance. The result may be much more elaborate terms in individuals agreements than the 1977 model would suggest – as witness the recent United States-Germany agreement. But the core, in the sense of the 1977 Model and Commentary, has been supplemented rather than superseded. In part, this is a recognition of the difficulties found in reaching even the 1977 modifications of the 1963 model.

402. It must also reflect the considerable and growing inertia of the double tax agreement system. As more states conclude more agreements, so renegotiation of the basic framework becomes progressively more difficult. A concession made to one state by another may result in third states seeking similar advantages. This will result in there being a strong disincentive for any individual state making a major movement at a unilateral level or for a state opening negotiations which may result in the need to revise its agreements in a manner that may prove adverse to its interests.

And the existence of machine-based collections of treaty texts makes it ever easier for states to monitor one anothers' practices.

403. Whilst this increasing stultification of the core of the OECD and UN models is perhaps unavoidable, it is in sharp distinction to the approach taken in some of the national reforms noted in the previous part of this report. Our objective in this part of the report is to explore the effects on international taxation of these national changes.

404. It may be that states are better disposed to agreeing the firm shape of a general revision of the model agreements in a few years' time. If so, what changes will it include? How would the tax reforms of the last two decades affect such a revision? Would there be other or better answers to the problems of international taxation? Is the answer to be found in developments such as the OECD/Council of Europe joint initiative in drafting the multilateral agreement on mutual assistance of revenue authorities? Are there, yet, any clear answers to the problems of international taxation or have the pressures not yet reached the point where decisions will occur?

405. An attempt to analyse the effects of recent changes on tax systems, and the contexts in which those changes occur, raises all the above questions, including the most fundamental. Whilst it is not our purpose to repeat the history of international taxation, or to explore each of these issues, it should be our aim that we investigate developments internationally in the same way as we reviewed national developments, in an attempt to identify any trends and changes, and also to identify any lack of direction behind developments. In considering these developments, some clarification is needed in this context into what there is to be developed – in other words, the scope of our subject.

The scope of double taxation

Double taxation can be viewed either from the point of view of a taxpayer or of a state's tax officials. From the point of view of a state the problems are:
the correct assertion of jurisdiction by a state of its tax laws over activities or persons which may be considered by the state as within the scope of its taxing laws;
the proper identification of the extent to which transactions or persons which are within that jurisdiction fall to be taxed under its laws;
where a transaction or person is or may be within the jurisdiction, the assertion of measures to prevent unacceptable avoidance of liability to that state's taxes;

where a transaction or person falls within the tax jurisdictions of that and of other taxing authorities, the assessment and collection of an acceptable share of the potential tax revenue by the authorities of each state;
the establishment of procedures to ensure that liabilities to tax are properly assessed, and that collection of tax revenues is efficiently achieved notwithstanding that this involves actions beyond the state's usual jurisdictional limits.

407. The usual assumption is that where there is a transaction proposed between two states both of which are maintaining full-tax policies and both of which regard themselves as appropriate taxing authorities and take no account of the other's claim, the resultant double tax bill is likely to deter taxpayers from undertaking that transaction in that form.

408. Where a taxing authority follows a low-tax policy, or is a tax haven, the problems outlined above become instead opportunities. There is only limited occasion for a full-tax taxing authority to use international double taxation to increase its revenue unless it is at the expense or potential expense of another state, but the reverse is clearly true for those using their choices of tax structures and related aspects of their legal systems to attract customers.

409. Viewed from the taxpayer's point of view, the problems and opportunities are those of any tax matter: firstly of compliance, including minimisation of compliance costs, and secondly of minimisation of tax costs including both the total tax costs and the cash-flow effects of tax liabilities.

410. These differing viewpoints emphasise that double taxation is a three-way conflict, rather than the two-way conflict of domestic taxation. This is because, although the two taxing authorities will have common cause to some extent against the taxpayer, they will also be in conflict in sharing the total tax revenues. Alternatively, where one of the tax authorities is a tax haven authority, it may have common cause with the taxpayer against the other tax authority whilst, of course, still seeking its own revenues from that taxpayer. In looking for trends, therefore, we need to concentrate on the inter-state developments as well as the developments noted in the first part of the report.

Growth of the problems

411. During the last two decades, as we have noted, all the evidence points to a continuing growth of international trade and cross-frontier transactions of all kinds at rates faster than the growth of gross national products. This includes a major growth in services provided international-

ly. There is also a rapid growth in the level and values of international financial transactions. The effect is that in most states the share of taxable activity involving an international element grows apace, as also does the number of company groups with an international element within them.

412. That is reinforced as economies open up their financial sectors either completely, or within much larger market (as in the Single European Market of the European Communities). This pressure has led to strongly protected economies like those of Russia and Brasil being opened up, in part for fear that otherwise they will become isolated from the increasing integration of the developed world's economies. Of itself, international double taxation is therefore steadily becoming more important to any tax system, as are the jurisdictional problems of a taxing authority.

413. Several other factors increase this growth in importance:

First, we have also noted the growth in low-tax or no-tax systems. It is now relatively easy for a taxpayer to structure affairs through a low-tax route if it so wishes, subject to the effects of 'outreach' provisions of other states.

Second, the revolutions in information and transport technologies. Transactions and procedures that were impossible a generation ago (when our present international taxation system was established) are now instantaneous, as with the transfer around the world not just of information but of financial instructions and therefore bank balances. Couriers and corporate officers can cross the oceans for the day returning that night. These advances are backed by equally irreversible advances in data-processing and other computer technologies that facilitate rapid financial deals of major magnitudes.

Third, (and facilitated by the second advance), we have the arrival of the truly international corporate organisation. Whilst MNCs (multi-national corporations) were possible once the corporation laws existed allowing them, the MNC can now be a truly international concern, with no one base for all its activities. Indeed, as is regularly observed, to talk of the residence of a corporate structure in MNC form is increasingly meaningless as a factual statement. The analogy with the residence of individuals breaks down and has not yet been replaced with alternative approaches based on location.

Fourth, and supporting the third development, corporate advisers are also increasingly international. The major firms of accountants and management consultants and, to a lesser extent, lawyers can now be as international as their clients, employing local advisory staff in any jurisdiction that is of significance.

Fifthly, and as an obvious extension from the changes already noted, markets are also being internationalised. Non-stop global trading in markets which shift around the globe as the globe itself shifts is already a reality. International market makers can, and do, operate in each of several locations on a continuing basis, in effect, the market being operated by shift workers, but with the shifts located in different continents.

Sixthly, and again following from those already noted, there has been an explosion in the knowledge about the differences between tax systems. Excellent summaries (such as those used in part in preparing this report) are readily available, and information about new developments anywhere in the world is widely disseminated and analysed. A recent illustration of this is the developments in Malta, and their marketing through MIBA. As perfect information is a precondition for a perfect market, an obvious effect in this increasingly easy availability of full information is a growth in competitiveness of national tax systems, and particularly in a shortened response time by taxpayers to changes in national tax systems. The ability to programme a database with the relevant information about every tax treaty and national tax system so that a computer can work out the optimum financial structure for a given international transaction, or the ability to put all the worlds' tax treaties on one CD-ROM, accessible through any personal computer, makes the study of technical comparative tax issues readily possible.

Seventhly, the pressures on national revenue authorities in recent years have forced them, as we have already noted, to pay more attention to international transactions. Whilst some time ago it would have been relatively inexpensive for a national tax authority to take a tolerant view of offshore arrangements, that is increasingly difficult both because of the relative share of national activity now involving an international aspect, and because of the deficits in finance being faced by many governments.

Eighthly, growing loosening of national restrictions against international free trade and transactions either on a regional or a fully international basis are having major effects on the mobility of goods, services and capital, though less so on free movement of workers for permanent or semi-permanent stays. In terms of goods, this involves the scaling down and dismantling of protective duty barriers, as has happened with a number of Asian, South American and East European states in recent years, and is being tackled by other protective economies such as Japan or Canada. In terms of capital, it arises from the abolition of exchange control regulations, for example in France and Italy as part of the development of the Single European Market for 1993.

Finally, and again we have already noted this, many responsible for national tax systems are finding it more difficult to develop their systems in isolation, or to change their systems from a set form of taxation. The trends noted in the first part of the report show a growing habit of imitation, and a growing convergence in shape, between national systems. As that happens, so the remaining differences are highlighted. If the difference is seen as a tax penalty to taxpayers, then the system may be avoided. If it is an advantage, clearly it will attract, but also may set in motion further downward spiralling of marginal tax costs.

414. This is of itself a remarkable development. Most states allow their laws to evolve slowly, and hold their own answers to particular problems – answers shaped strongly by a long history of evolution, or by the traumas of particular historic episodes. The relevance of the answers used by other countries is limited, and comparative legal study is an esoteric interest. This is now only true to a limited extent of commercial and trade laws, where common forms are being refined steadily. It has ceased to be true for tax laws.

Common forms of taxation

415. In tax, or at least in some parts of it, the move to world-wide common forms is – in world historical terms – precipitous in its speed. The world has adopted VAT as a tax in not much more time than it has taken the English law reform authorities to codify *in draft* our own criminal laws without attempting very much by way of reform in the process! In no other area of national law will so much common ground in legal forms be found straddling the divides of common law, civil law or the other main legal traditions, or so much interest be evident in what other states are doing and intending to do, or jurisdictional limits of a national law system be more tested.

416. This pressure to adopt external patterns is enhanced where a state faces external financial pressures. Forms of taxation become the subject of external advice and recommendations, for example from the World Bank or IMF, where a state seeks international assistance. This is reflected in national reforms introduced as part of an agreement with external lenders, as featured in recent publications of both the World Bank and the IMF. If such moves put an adverse pressure on states which decide to seek divergent forms of raising tax finance, the pressure to seek the safe haven

of patterns of taxation acceptable in more influential states will remain strong. This pressure has been evidenced recently in Europe, as the eastern European states seek to join the capitalist world, and in Africa where states like Kenya seek to deal with external debt, and in South America where attempts are made to tackle inflationary pressures.

417. Nor is it at the state level that this interest in comparative study stops. As we noted in the previous section, there are several 'best-sellers' among books which give short synopses of national systems on a comparative basis, or present a 'tax tour' of some particular area of the globe or sector of the world economy. These works are reflections of the interest of both taxpayers and their advisers in seeking sufficient levels of knowledge both for compliance and useful planning to ensure an effective tax strategy.

418. Here again, the analogy with other areas of law is worth a moment's thought. Clearly, many areas of a state's laws will concern the international corporation little. It will have to comply with local laws which impinge directly on its activities, but only to a limited extent. It can ensure its contracts are governed by a chosen system of law (or by rules made up for the purpose), and that its disputes are tried by a court of its choice (or, again, by the neutral forum of an arbitration). It can use the lawyers of any state it chooses for its contract negotiations. Tax is, along with the relevant criminal laws, about the only aspect of a third state's laws which cannot be avoided.

419. These factors suggest an increasing significance in any state's national tax system both to its international aspects and to a comparative assessment of its techniques and policies. It also suggests, we argue, some of the reasons for the current spate of reform. To the extent that a state has an open economy, it is not cnough for it to adjust its double taxation arrangements in order to be competitive (as may once have been the case). It must adjust its full systems and, perhaps psychologically just as important, be seen to be doing so.

420. This has been evidenced not just in VAT but in other changes in national systems. We have noted strong national reasons why new kinds of tax are unusual. But a further reason is the international complication of changing from a well-tried basis of tax. For example, one reason cited against both an expenditure tax (to replace an income tax) and a cash-flow based corporation tax is the difficulty of fitting such a new tax in with existing international agreements and other states' systems. The existing structure places a practical limit on the extent of future divergences from

usual practice. The stronger the pressures to convergence now are, the harder it will be for non-consensual changes to occur.

421. It also imposes a strong pressure towards convergences both in the tax base and the tax rates of established taxes except where a state seeks deliberately to create some special feature to its tax system. Even these special features – be it a no-tax regime such as that of the Cayman Islands, or a bid to handle particular kinds of business as with some other tax havens or low-tax countries – are now chosen with an eye to the international market place rather than internal developments. This again can clearly be seen in the way smaller states approach the designs of their systems. Thus, thinking in states like Malta and Poland is concentrated on how they can conform to the overall pattern whilst creating a competitive edge in some aspect of the whole.

422. Arguably, only the United States and Japan of the Group of Seven can stand aside from current trends, if they wish. They have not done so. The United States has, rather, been in the forefront of changes, whilst the Japanese – with some uncertainty – have also been involved in tax reform. The European members cannot stand aside because of developments within the European Communities. And because, therefore, the whole Group of Seven are involved in reviewing and adjusting their tax systems, few others can afford to stand aside if they wish to take part in the same economic activities as the developed states.

International responses

423. Given that the strongest economies have been influenced in this way, how have states generally responded to these pressures and influences? The extent to which states have themselves adopted the 'MNC' format is, so far, minimal. That is, we have seen little successful adoption of a level of multi-national taxing competencies, or inter-state grouping, equivalent to the structure of a corporate group. Very slowly, the European Communities are moving toward common forms and solutions, against the individual state veto in the Single European Act. At the same time one other experiment in common forms – that of the CMEA or COMECON, the commercial form of the Warsaw Pact – has disintegrated.

424. The failure to find easy multinational solutions is hardly surprising, given the juridical nature of a state, and the political realities within most nations. A study of the continuing relevance of the classical concept of an omnicompetent sovereign state is outside the scope of this thesis. It may, however, be observed in passing that taxation is central to any governmental process. If, as we argue, individual states are losing the ability to

shape their tax policies because the pressures on the state are too great to allow it a truly free choice in tax policies, this must be of relevance to a contemporary examination of what is meant by a 'state' and 'sovereignty'.

425. It is interesting that there has been a long history of attempts to form cross-frontier taxing competencies through the mechanism of common markets and economic unions. The European Communities is the one body that has gone further than a customs union or free trade area in terms of substantive taxation. In 1991, it is poised not only to consider several applications to swell its membership from twelve, but also to reach important agreements with the six members of EFTA and it is starting the same process with other European states. Outside Western Europe and aside from customs law, other agreements have been attempted but have had only faltering progress. More progress has been made with inter-governmental agreements on assistance, such as the Nordic agreement, and those like-minded states also have a multilateral tax agreement. Elsewhere, despite strong pressure on national finances and strong taxpayer pressures, states have failed to agree even on an independent form of international dispute settlement.

426. The most obvious effect of the absence of action by states to seek positive cooperation has been in connection with the tax reform process itself. Several policy commentators have drawn attention – in international fora as well as individually – to the challenge presented to states by current reforms, and the opportunity for cooperative responses. Instead, we have seen responses that are either uncoordinated or competitive. The most that can be said about coordination is that states do share both experience and ideas so that decisions can be taken with full awareness of their international contexts.

427. Solutions have therefore either been national or by bilateral treaty, the process varying from one kind of tax to another. A major development of the last decade has been in the parallel national developments of techniques to deal with offshore arrangements associated, in the view of a state, with its taxpayers. The one 'international' development has been in the adoption and renegotiation of bilateral agreements, which we will note first.

Developments in international agreements

(1) *DTAs*

428. From the first agreements between European states to the present structure of international direct tax agreements is a period of about a century. During that time the growth of use of agreements, initially very slow,

has been exponential. This is partly because the number of states has itself sharply increased during the last 25 years as the winds of change blew away colonial structures. It is also a reflection of the growth in bilateral trading relations between states, and of the necessity to solve the jurisdictional and overlap problems caused by double tax.

429. The pace was accelerated by adoption of the OECD common form of double taxation convention on income and capital in 1963, and its revision in 1977. This was followed by agreement on a common form of convention for estate and gifts taxes. This is not least because those DTAs formed an agreed agenda for bilateral discussions, and has also been the basis for both multilateral (the UN version), regional (the ASEAN and Andean models) and unilateral (the US and Netherlands versions, amongst others) variants used as the basis for international discussions. In this sense, the OECD models have proved fertile sources of individual agreements, whilst not being agreements themselves.

430. During the last few years, the networks of DTAs have continued to grow apace, as evidenced by the lengthy list in each year's Annual Report of the International Bureau for Fiscal Documentation. Within the OECD the network is now moving towards completion, with some states (including the UK) now having comprehensive agreements with all other members. There have been a series of agreements between western European and eastern European states, between OECD states and China and also India, and generally between the developed and developing world. The United States, which has traditionally seen only limited values in DTAs, has extended its network. Where previously there were limited agreements (often covering international transportation alone) full double tax conventions are being substituted, the overall total of agreements now approaching 900.

431. The one area where the network, never substantial, has declined is in the revocation by a number of advanced states, led by the United States, of tax treaties with tax havens, such as the Netherlands Antilles. Even here negotiated replacements are occurring, albeit on terms more in the interests of the advanced economies.

432. With this limited exception, the network is likely to continue growing simply because of the momentum of previous growth. It is interesting, in that respect, to note the importance states seem to be attaching to the existence or negotiation of DTAs with Poland and its neighbours as part of the programme to expand trade with those states. It appears that DTAs now have a value in themselves as part of the formal relationships between two friendly states.

433. We discuss in the next chapter the contents of those agreements and the extent to which the individual DTAs follow the models. We may note for the present that the most important conclusion is that states do pay close attention to the models, and that both form and content of most agreements substantially repeats those of the models.

The scope for multilateral agreements
434. Despite the above conclusion suggesting scope for a multilateral taxation treaty, attempts to negotiate one, or even find common ground for one, have so far foundered with only one group of exceptions. That is the series of multilateral taxation agreements concluded by the Nordic states of Denmark, Finland, Iceland, Norway, and Sweden. This development was significantly strengthened by the agreement of a new multilateral DTA on incomes and net worth in 1989, bringing the Faroe Islands within the scope of the treaties, and supported by a new multilateral estates and gifts tax DTA to replace existing bilateral agreements. These are both also supported by a multilateral assistance treaty between the same states, making the composite framework the most advanced international cooperation in direct taxes yet achieved.

435. It is worth noting that the absence of other multilateral agreements is not because of any absence of desire for such an agreement. Indeed, it should be recorded that a number of at times strenuous attempts have been made to reach agreement on a regional basis on a common form of multilateral agreement. One such attempt has been through the agency of the European Communities, and another through the auspices of the European Free Trade Association before some of its member state left to join the Communities. In at least one case the pace of discussion was intensive, with regular weekly meetings, and a detailed clause by clause examination of possible texts. But the key ingredient of political will to agree was absent.

436. The texts of the two multilateral Nordic double tax treaties show the strong influence of the bilateral treaties that they replaced, and, behind them, the work of the OECD of which all five states are members. There are no major new concepts or approaches in these agreements, which in some clauses resort to lists to cover the differences between the treaty partners. But they have shown that, given a common cultural and economic background, genuine multilateral cooperation on an evolving basis is achievable.

437. Notably, the European Communities Treaties refrained from giving the European Commission any express competence in this area, the matter being left by Article 220 of the EEC Treaty with member states.

Attempts to reach multilateral agreement within the Communities have been attempted but have so far failed to establish any strong will for any comprehensive agreement despite a lengthy search by groups of experts. Similar discussions in past years looking for common ground for a multilateral agreement between the EFTA countries also failed.

438. However, the impetus of the Single European market is reinforcing the will to introduce the first directives of a nature that will affect potential double tax liabilities of taxpayers. Particularly important, in terms of principle, is the proposal, emanating from 1969 but only agreed politically in 1990, for compulsory arbitration between member states where a taxpayer suffers double taxation as a result of inconsistent adjustments between states for transfer pricing. This was one of three relevant heads of agreement which were turned into the 'French package' of reforms adopted in mid-1990. It finally took the form not of a Community directive but of a draft multilateral convention which appears to count as an agreement within Article 220 for Community purposes, but like a bilateral treaty at national level. Along with this were agreements on the withholding taxes permissible on dividends between subsidiary and parent companies within the Community, and measures to stop excessive taxation on cross-border mergers and similar corporate changes. The Commission also announced a proposal that all withholding taxes on interest and royalties should be abolished between Community states, and that losses should be freely transferable.

439. These proposals will, if adopted, override several provisions in bilateral DTAs between Community states. In so doing, they might upset the balance on which some of the DTAs were agreed. If so, the Community will become, if indirectly, centrally involved in the DTAs of its members. That must, at some point, happen. Further, any most favoured nation clauses, or similar agreements or negotiating positions, will lead to these advantages also being secured by non-Community states. If that happens, the transferability of profits and losses, the reductions of withholdings and the adoption of arbitration now being agreed within the Community could in due course make significant differences to the present patterns of agreements.

440. Secondary procedural agreements are also being adopted, such as the agreements between the Nordic states on mutual assistance, with which Germany is also associated, and the provisions, adopted by directives, between the Community's member states.

441. However, the controversial draft produced jointly by the OECD and the Council of Europe opening the prospect of official cooperation

for all taxes save customs duties and between all the states of the OECD (and thereby including the twelve states of the European Community) and the Council of Europe (thereby including also all the other states of Western Europe) has attracted only limited support, and a number of direct refusals to sign. At the time of writing, the United States has indicated that it will ratify a limited part of the treaty (but also that it finds another part unconstitutional), and some of the Nordic states have also indicated support, Norway being the first state to ratify. On the other hand the United Kingdom and Luxembourg both indicated early dissent, as did Germany, thereby preventing a full international approach even within the Community.

442. The OECD/CE draft appears to have gone too far at the present state of development of cooperation between states in tax matters. Even some of its supporters (such as the USA) support only parts of what it covers. In attempting to tackle issues relating to all taxes apart from customs duties, and several administrative aspects of those taxes at once, it was over-ambitious whilst yet not providing adequate safeguards to counteract so major an advance.

443. That statement must be made against a background of growing cooperation between states on other parallel matters. In particular, there is a sustained tradition of cooperation within the member states of the Council of Europe in criminal matters, such as exchange of evidence, extradition of suspects and acceptance of convictions by courts. This has been adopted more widely in recent initiatives such as the United Nations Conventions on Psychotropic Substances. These agreements have led states to reach new levels of official cooperation, for example, in the use of search and seizure powers which go as far as equivalent provisions in the CE/OECD draft. Reticence in adopting that draft therefore reflects reticence as to the objectives at which the measures in the draft are aimed, rather than the procedures it employs.

(2) *Customs agreements*

444. Separately from this series of agreements have been three others groups of agreements, largely ignored in viewing overall tax developments. First are the agreements on customs duties and other border taxes and international transactions taxes, based around the Common Customs Convention (including mutual assistance agreements such as the recent agreement between France and Finland) and the agreements on customs valuation, and separately the General Agreement on Tariffs and Trades and the agreements subsidiary to it.

445. The advances here – often ignored by those commenting on international direct tax – make moves on direct tax seem cautious. Whilst GATT provisions tend to be a matter of high-level diplomacy, the Customs agreements on procedures, valuations, nomenclatures, temporary movements and other practical issues can be worked by customs authorities direct. So much is this so in some states that the departments of government responsible for customs law – supposedly the guardians of the frontiers – are the most internationally minded parts of government. These mechanisms are also more advanced than direct tax provisions in providing dispute resolution procedures on a multilateral basis. This is illustrated by the publication in 1990 by the European Commission not only of consolidations of customs law, but also a draft Common Customs Code, most of the provisions of which are already in force. The one new area is a proposed compulsory appeal system. It is also illustrated by the practice of dispute examination and resolution through GATT panels.

446. Less dramatic, but sometimes to important effect, are the free trade areas, such as the agreements between the European Communities and third states, EFTA, LAFTA and the more recent US-Canada free trade area. Whilst these may only provide tax-free trade in specific areas such as manufactured goods, they again provide international mechanisms which encourage states to develop practical approaches and dispute resolution techniques in taxation matters.

(3) *Social security agreements*

447. The second group are the multilateral and bilateral measures on social security taxes. These are usually by-products of agreements on social security benefit provision and come in two forms. First are the multilateral agreements and initiatives of and based on the drafts worked out through the auspices of the International Labour Organisation. Second are the bilateral agreements, to some extent using similar forms to DTAs (for example using the competent authority mechanisms and modified common forms of wording) which are slowly being adopted by developed states. For example, the United Kingdom now has 17 such agreements with other states outside the EC – although it has been hesitant to adopt some of them because of the potential cost to our social security systems.

(4) *Diplomatic and consular agreements*

448. The third area is that of the wider consular agreement, such as most favoured nation clauses or Treaties of Friendship, Commerce and Navigation or Investment Protection Agreements, including non-discrimination provisions. Unlike other kinds of agreement these are of little benefit in practical tax disputes. This is because there is no competent authority

procedure for these agreements, which are therefore governed by the formal procedures of diplomatic agreements. Provisions cannot be invoked direct by individuals or corporations in most states, but only through the external relations department of their own government. Representations will, therefore, inevitably be coloured by interests of state. Additional complications also arise with the question of recognition of the interests of a foreign parent company with a domestic subsidiary. As has happened before the US courts, a foreign parent may be ruled to have no standing in a dispute involving its local subsidiary.

449. There are also special agreements dealing with the tax status of diplomatic and consular officials (under the two Vienna Conventions), visiting foreign armed forces units and members, foreign heads of state and of government, embassies and headquarters of international organisations, plus the internal tax regimes applying, for example, within the United Nations and the European Communities.

450. Mention may also be made here of the growing network of agreements on aspects of criminal law and procedure. The network of multilateral agreements was noted earlier in this chapter. In practice it is also supported by a series of bilateral agreements on issues such as extradition and prisoner exchange, and is underwritten by relevant provisions in human rights provisions such as the European Convention on Human Rights. These provisions are relevant, inter alia, in connection with the enforcement of tax laws through the criminal processes. It means that the framework for inter-governmental cooperation on issues of tax avoidance finds a direct equivalent in provisions allowing similar cooperation in questions of tax evasion. Indeed, in some states it would seem there is more readiness to accept that there should be cooperation against evasion than against avoidance.

(5) *Other areas of substantive tax*

451. For indirect internal taxes there are hardly any international agreements. There are none, for example, concerning VAT outside the European Communities and limited management agreements such as that linking the United Kingdom and Manx value added taxes. There are hardly any dealing with other forms of indirect tax such as excises, though there are some agreements dealing with frontier purchases.

(6) *Facilitative organisations*

More generally, note must be taken of the international bodies which facilitate developments in these areas. There are the various forms of common market, customs union and free trade area covered above, but also supported by the GATT secretariat, the Fiscal Affairs Committee and Department of the OECD, a body which has undertaken considerable work on a very regular basis and to marked effect, the UN specialist committees and bodies (although little has come from UNCTAD) including the World Bank and the International Monetary Fund, both of which have developed specialist tax competencies and repeatedly funded private initiatives and missions to governments. Less prominently there are bodies such as the Commonwealth Association of Tax Administrators.

453. Private bodies, notably of course the International Fiscal Association and the associated International Bureau of Fiscal Documentation, and other bodies such as the International Chamber of Commerce should not be ignored in this context, as they have a major role to play in education, in representation and in the formulation of views and approaches. What is more, these bodies, like the governmental bodies, have grown considerably in breadth, experience and importance in the last two decades.

Extent of international coordination

454. The picture is therefore much more complex than the framework of DTAs taken by itself, complex though that now is, suggests. This complexity is itself a development of note, though one to which little attention as such has been paid. For this ever-growing network has to comply at each stage with treaty law and diplomatic requirements, as well as internal considerations. It is clear that most states now regard the conclusion of double tax conventions as worthwhile achievements, and as part of the pattern of relationships with trading partners. It is also clear that a developed state will find itself a party to several dozen tax treaties of several kinds. Nonetheless, the pattern is still only a partial one, as can be judged by the number of conventions necessary to form a complete network :

Complete between all EC states:	66
Complete between all OECD states:	276
Complete between all 185 economies recognised by the World Bank:	16,820

This exercise in listing possibilities shows just how important a clear structure of international tax relationships is, even within groups of states with some similarity of economies and goals. On a total global scale ability to operate within a growing network of international agreements will require a very strong underlying structure if the network is to be workable even by the most acute advisers to states or taxpayers.

455. One other simple piece of mathematics makes this point. The number of possible three-way trading links (ie combinations of transactions involving the linking of two separate DTAs) will be at present about 40,000 (assuming 900 DTAs, any one of which may be linked with any other). At the extreme of a full set of DTAs between all economies currently functioning, that number becomes over 140 million. The number of four-way links possible on that extreme basis (that is, chains of three DTAs) would be somewhere approaching a trillion – 1,000,000,000,000. Granted that the number of DTA is likely to stay far short of the possible total for many years, nonetheless the mathematics makes the point that interactions between two, three or four economies through unstructured DTAs would rapidly lead to a bewildering (and in practical terms, infinite) range of possibilities.

456. The conclusion of a DTA is not, however, the end of the problem. The agreements are not comprehensive, and many of their terms are open to doubt as to precise content. Aside from any doubts as to the meaning of a treaty provision, there is the basic question of when it is in force, and to what extent. These questions will steadily become more important as advisers in different countries become more familiar with the problems.

457. The proliferation of DTAs also begs the question we address in the next chapter, namely what purpose is served by a DTA or similar agreement. That seems to have received little public attention, as does the separate question noted at the head of this chapter about the relevance of the form of agreement to changing tax structures. The form of agreement adopted is invariably a modified form of the OECD/UN model.

Treaty overrides

458. A more recent development is the possibility of a failure of a state to apply a DTA to its full extent. This will depend both on the constitutional structure of a state, and on its domestic tax law. Of particular concern to many major companies and, through representations, to the Council of the OECD, have been some recent United States 'treaty override' provisions. This is of concern not just to individual taxpayers which may be caught by the new branch profits tax, but because of two issues of principle. First is that this compromises the integrity of individual DTAs, and adds complexity to an already difficult legal position. Second, it challenges the purpose of an international treaty per se. In addition, there is the practical issue of charting the precise rules operating between two states. If one has to check whether the DTA, where one exists, does or does not operate to override national rules, a new dimension of complexity is added to those already present.

459. The International Chamber of Commerce, in a 1987 Symposium, agreed that:

> The branch level tax is the wrong approach: it is detrimental to international trade and investment. It could require a total re-evaluation of doing business in the U.S. for non-U.S. enterprises although this would be precluded by most tax treaties. Many complexities and unanswered questions remain with respect to the addition of this provision to the U.S. Code. The foreign tax credit provisions have been made more restrictive and complicated beyond any necessity. But, as fiscal considerations are not the only ones to be taken into account, some high-tax countries will remain attractive if they provide good business opportunities, and it is expected that U.S. investors will manoeuvre within the new rules rather than pull out of high – tax countries.
>
> The international business community is concerned about tendencies toward promoting isolationism and protectionism in tax relationships among the world's trading partners.

460. Since then, the Council of the OECD has also taken a clear position on this issue. Treaty overrides are perhaps most charitably seen as the extreme extent of measures felt necessary by an increasing number of states to deal unilaterally with international tax avoidance issues directly affecting them. They come about through particular circumstances. First is a constitutional point, namely that it is permissible within the state for a treaty provision to be overridden in any way – this is not always so, and may place some states at a disadvantage to others because of their internal constitutional arrangements. Second is that the real concern in treaty override cases is the dispute between the state and the taxpayer. The second state becomes drawn into this as a separate issue. If and insofar as the treaty override is primarily aimed at affecting the revenue share between the two states parties, rather than protecting the first state's revenue against particular activities by a taxpayer, a different level of dispute arises. In comments made to us by informed US observers, we have found some embarrassment about treaty overrides and an anxiety that they be not seen as inter-state conflicts.

461. It would be wrong to depict the US federal authorities as the only 'overriders'. For one thing, the practice is not that of the federal tax authorities or of the executive arm of government. Rather, it is a reflection of a wider problem in the United States arising from the clear separation of powers applying to international obligations. This leaves with the President and the House the issues of taxation to be adjusted within a double

tax agreement, whilst the Senate is required to advise and consent on all treaties regardless of content.

462. There are constitutional questions in other states about the extent to which treaties may be overridden. There are also measures, such as those in the UK Finance Act 1989, where section 115 purports to define by unilateral legislation the content of bilateral agreements and also the measures on dual residents, which appear to some to encroach on treaty concepts. At the same time, there are the 'overrides' present in indirect taxation with the failure of member states of the European Communities to comply with their obligations under Community law, as witness the cases on failure to implement the VAT directives in full.

463. Clearly this tendency to dilute the effects of international agreements must be taken into account in assessing the extent of international cooperation. It is important rather less of itself, and rather more in the extent to which it might indicate that states regard double tax agreements (and similar) as some kind of second class legal obligation which does not have to be respected fully by a national law system. But, one must ask, if DTAs do not have the full force of an international treaty, what force do they have? We are not concerned here with treaties laying down political objectives for action, or common targets which rarely affect other states parties, but rules which enter the practical relationships of any taxpayer whose activities extend beyond the frontiers of one state.

464. Given that the pressures to build a world-wide network of DTAs and similar agreements must impose substantial limits on any state, pressures to engage in treaty overriding are likely to grow if individual states find themselves under budgetary pressure to increase tax revenues. As, almost by definition, that pressure will constantly be present in many states, so will the pressure to engage in some form of override of inconvenient or expensive aspects of treaties, unless it is counteracted by pressures against the principle or practices of overrides. Overriding may not, of course, always appear as a legislative dissent. Rather, it may take the form of a highly bureaucratic and slow mechanism to obtain what becomes long-delayed relief from a withholding tax, or in a self-serving interpretation of a provision which it proves difficult to have reviewed, or measures which intercept a transaction before it becomes taxable internationally.

465. The strength of both governmental and taxpayer reaction to the federal branch profits tax imposed by the United States suggests, as argued above, that there is considerable sensitivity to actions seen as treaty abuse not as an unwarranted exercise of sovereignty but as a matter of fair dealing. The compromises now being reached on the issue through adjust-

ments to double tax agreements, also suggest that the action was seen as offending against the principles which underlie double tax agreements as much as the terms of individual agreements. Whilst the constitutional arrangements for making tax laws in the United States means that foreign pressures may be of less significance than in some other states, the existence of the pressure affirms the importance of the values noted above.

466. Another, more insidious, form of treaty override comes when a court of one state party adopts an interpretation of a DTA which is inconsistent with that in the other party, or to the jointly expressed approach of the two competent authorities. The recent UK case of *Commerzbank* and *Banco do Brasil* illustrates this. Unless a court is sensitive to the views of competent authorities (as are the US courts), there is a danger that the use of courts may cause divergences which will not be anticipated by taxpayers of the other state or third states. This is particularly so if a divergence concerns interpretation of a provision in the form of an OECD model article. In the absence of some agreed and effective bilateral or multilateral disputes procedures, the possibility of such divergences remains significant.

The future framework

467. Negotiation of a new double tax agreement is increasingly an exercise with fixed procedures, a fixed agenda, a series of accepted concepts and alternatives, and a partially predetermined outcome. Important differences still appear in newly negotiated treaties, but the inertia imposed on officials by the existing body of treaties and the common models is such that the approaches and responses fall within a well known pattern.
This does not mean that such agreements are inevitable. The United Kingdom, despite the extent of its network, has failed to find sufficient common interest with some potential treaty partners (for example, Brasil). In other cases treaties negotiated to the apparent satisfaction of the competent authorities are only accepted much later – or even not at all – by the legislative and executive authorities with the states parties. And in other cases again one side may think it has reached an agreement which the other side does not accept has been agreed. It is understood, for example, that the United Kingdom authorities thought that their agreement negotiated with the Ghanaian authorities in 1977 had taken effect, but that the Ghanaian authorities thought otherwise, and continued to abide by their 1947 agreement. But the general rule is that agreements are concluded and implemented in a common form to an ever-growing extent.

468. Once a double tax agreement is in place, the temptation is to expand it to a fully comprehensive agreement along the lines of the models. Once

those models have been adopted, the inertia of the system will make it difficult to break away from the established pattern. This may be because there may be a fear by one or both of the parties that the bargain, even if not a good one, can only be replaced by a worse bargain. A notorious example of failing to reach a better bargain must be the United States – Netherlands agreement, which predates even the 1963 OECD model. At the same time, there will be limited situations in which no treaty is better than a bad one. The special cases of the termination of treaties with the Netherlands Antilles show that this may occasionally be the preferred course, but the exceptional nature of those terminations shows that this will rarely be so. The revocation of any DTA mitigating withholding taxes between two major financial partners would raise the risk of massive reroutings of funds and serious economic side-effects which are unlikely to be risked by many.

469. Procedures exist, of course, to modify DTAs by protocols and notes. These are, however, full international agreements in their own right and do not happen lightly. It is equally possible to build into the agreements terms under which adjustments can be made on any change in the system without the need for new negotiations (as the West German agreements have tried), but these are not common.

470. The conclusion must be that there is considerable inertia in the double tax agreement system, both in the form and content of individual agreements, and the perpetuation of agreements once they have been concluded.

471. A similar answer must be given to the treaty frameworks relating to other forms of tax. The Uruguay Round of negotiations of GATT may have been arduous and may yet fail, but the negotiations have been truly international and have embraced a significantly extended scope of operation, and they have led to serious talk both of the conversion of GATT to a permanent international organisation and of the creation of a parallel general agreement on services which, sooner or later, will prove acceptable. Customs procedures have reached a state of coordination which it is difficult to see being reversed. In short, the future of tax coordination in these areas as in direct taxes has now taken a shape which it is difficult to see changing in any major way without the most significant of initiatives. And there seems little in the current world situation to give rise to such initiatives for change. Changes will therefore take place, if at all, by an evolution within and from existing structures.

Conclusion

472. The above review suggests that, for direct taxation, the main method for dealing with double taxation of income, gains and other direct taxes for the foreseeable future will be through the medium of a double tax convention based directly or indirectly on the format of the 1977 OECD model and the concepts and approaches employed therein, with limited flexibility in terms of updating individual treaties once agreed. Indirect taxes are divided between VAT which has, as we shall explore further, an inbuilt adjustment to international transactions in its present structure, and other tariff and trade taxes for which there is an even more firmly established international regime. Although all forms of cooperation will be of increased importance in all areas, it will be increasingly difficult to change fundamentally these approaches to the problems of international double taxation and international transaction and trade taxes. At the same time, the scope for reducing these bilateral agreements to agreed international codes and broad multilateral agreements is limited to the indirect taxes or to specific regions with strong common interests.

473. Unilateral actions of developed states in extending their tax jurisdictions through what we termed outreach provisions, and the recent spate of reforms to all aspects of national tax systems, both suggest that the structural frameworks of the tax systems on the basis of which these treaty answers evolved are seen at the national level as flawed and in need of improvement. We must now examine how far the established frameworks are seen as adequate for the revised tasks that they are to perform in the light of tax reforms, and we attempt to do this by a qualitative examination, followed by a limited attempt at a quantitative examination, before examining what conclusions can be drawn.

Chapter 5

Tackling double taxation

Can two walk together, except they be agreed?
The Book of Amos

500. It is usually assumed that measures granting double taxation relief are aimed at relieving double taxation on a taxpayer. That may seem a trite thought with which to start this part of the discussion, but the point must be made – and will be explored below – that in practice that may not be the sole aim, or even the major objective, of particular measures. Just as there are taxes designed *not* to collect tax (prohibitive import and export duties are two relevant examples) so it should not be assumed that double tax measures are necessarily designed to help the taxpayer.

501. If an examination of double taxation relief cannot assume that objective, thought needs to be given to alternative objectives, and to the conceptual framework within which double taxation relief must operate. A second starting point must also be noted, deriving added significance from trends noted earlier in this study. This is that a proper discussion of double taxation must comprehend all forms of taxation, and reflect the shift away from personal direct taxes on narrow bases to wider bases and to wider use of comprehensive indirect taxes, social security taxes and local taxes.

502. In this chapter, after clarifying what we mean by double taxation, we look at the legal bases on which taxing competence can be claimed, and changes occurring in the use of those bases. We examine how recent changes in the forms and rates of tax used by states have influenced the location of taxing competence. We then turn to the question of double tax relief, and attempt some assessment of changes there.

An objective for double taxation relief

503. It may be stated as a basis for comment that double tax relief, if it is effective and genuinely has tax relief of the taxpayer as its objective, should achieve the situation where the taxpayer pays no more tax operating cross-border than it would if operating in one state alone. In other words, the system should be neutral to the decision to operate cross-bor-

der. As has long been recognised in the distinction between capital export neutrality and capital import neutrality, even this statement cannot be made without qualification.

504. A company operating from State A into State B (or the reverse) has three comparators – the companies operating in their home markets in both states, and a cross-border operator in the reverse direction. If State A has higher tax than State B, to which system should the cross-border operators be neutral: the state from which they operate, the state to which they operate, or each other? Relating that to the point made above, neutrality may also be sought either within individual taxes or within the system as a whole. Neutrality has been an objective of internal tax reforms over recent years. It remains to examine whether this objective has been pursued internationally. For it to have been achieved, there must be either less chance of double taxation arising, or a greater degree of double tax relief.

505. Double taxation arises when more than one state claims competence to tax a single person or transaction. To see if there have been any changes in the potential for double tax, we must note not only the rules operating to determine tax base and tax rate, but also the extent of jurisdictional claims to tax. For it is only if states adopt the same, non-overlapping, tests of jurisdiction to tax that double taxation will cease to occur.

1 THE LEGAL COMPETENCE TO TAX

A legal framework for tackling double taxation

506. Doctrine provides several fully coherent answers to the question of how neutrality should be achieved. Practice provides no single overall approach. What emerges is a second best answer: that a cross-border operator should not pay more tax than any of the comparators, in other words, tax should not act as a penalty on cross-border operations unless, as with export and import taxes, that penalty is deliberate.

507. In deciding whether this second best answer is the 'right' answer, the decision-maker must wittingly or otherwise decide what kind of decision (in the sense of the kind of law being handled) is being taken. Because of inconsistencies of attitude this is itself not clear; it could be public or private law. Taxation law, at least in its jurisdictional application is public law, as is criminal law and, for example, regulatory laws about health or employment. Problems of conflict between tax laws of different states are therefore matters of international public law, and answers to the conflict form part of the corpus of that law.

508. At the same time, the individual contents of tax laws more often resemble private law, with taxation depending on the 'true' nature of a contract for trade or employment, or the precise terms of a gift or the powers of a legal person such as a trust. Here any conflict will be a matter not of public law but of private law, and will be resolved by the well-developed rules of international private law or 'conflicts of law'.

509. This inconsistency may lead to an inconsistency in identifying individuals with tax systems. For example, the rules dealing with succession to property on death where more than one legal system is involved are determined by rules of conflicts of law in the private domain. These identify with the 'domicile' of the individual – itself determined by conflicts rules designed to locate the permanent home of that individual. It is on those rules which the rules of international double taxation of property passing on succession by death are largely based.

510. The assertion of the public laws of a state can occur in a number of internationally recognised ways, chief of which are territorial assertion and personal assertion over nationals of the state. States have therefore a multiple choice of basis on which to tax, depending on the adoption, first, of a public or a private approach to the question and, second, to the basis for assertion of jurisdiction even as a matter of international public law. The choice is widened by the availability to a state of a variety of means of raising taxes with different jurisdictional rules applying to the different taxes. The second best answer noted above results from an absence of a consistent choice internationally between these fundamentally different approaches to the question of jurisdictional competence.

The assertion of territorial sovereignty

511. One approach to asserting taxing competence assumes that the authority to tax is essentially an attribute of territorial sovereignty. This reflects the core idea of a modern nation state as a territory with its 'own' government – a concept which lies at the heart of modern international public law. A state, because of its status, has power to impose its public laws (though it does not follow that this is true of private laws such as family law or the laws of succession) over all its territory. It therefore has the right to impose taxation over all assets, persons and transactions in its territory subject only to exceptions recognised by international public law as limitations on the powers of a state (such as diplomatic immunities and treaty-based limits). The consequence of this doctrine is that a state can impose taxes on any activity by any taxpayer within its territorial scope, regardless of the extent of the connection of the taxpayer with the state.

512. This approach is the general approach to indirect taxes, subject to one problem: where does a transaction occur? In particular, if the cross-border transaction is the sale of goods or services, does the sale occur at the seller's end, at the buyer's end or at the place where (either by agreement between the two parties, or as a result of the operation of the international private law of contract) the contract is concluded? If it is the provision of capital, again where is the loan or credit located? The growth in the use of value added taxes, and the sharp increase on cross-border capital flows, make these points of much greater importance than even a few decades ago.

513. The choice of claim is clearly evidenced by a cross-border sales tax of the value added tax kind. Should the tax be collected in the state where the goods or services are produced – the state of origin – or the state where they are received and consumed – the state of destination, or on some other basis? The European Communities have adopted a consumer-based, and therefore destination-based, pattern of VAT in order to create neutrality of taxation of consumption.

514. The Commission has sought to get this changed to an origin-based tax. Its 1990 proposals affirm 1996 as the year when the system will be changed to an origin basis throughout the Community if their view as to change is accepted, but little enthusiasm is evidenced amongst the member states for such a change. They have so far agreed only to look at the matter again before 1997. Meanwhile most other states adopting a VAT have copied the EC approach, and gone for a consumption-based tax. If the Community does change the basis of its tax, and other states do not, serious problems will occur by way of double taxation or double failure to tax. As at mid-1990 the Commission had no public views on solutions to this issue.

515. In connection with direct taxes, basing a claim to tax on the location of the activity is usually labelled the 'source state' approach in double taxation debates, that is, the state where the source of the taxable income/wealth arises is the state with taxing competence. For direct taxes, though not necessarily for indirect taxes, the source may be where the money is derived from, not where the contract is made. In VAT terms, the 'source' state in this sense is, for VAT purposes, the destination state (this apparent semantic conflict is because the destination of the goods is the source of the cash to pay for them).

516. The source basis is widely asserted as an appropriate basis for direct taxes also. It is recognised by the OECD and UN model double taxation

treaties in respect of many forms of income: income from land or immovables, profits of permanent establishments of a business in a territory, dividends, interest and (in the case of the UN model) royalties paid from a territory and employments within a territory.
517. The assertion of the source basis to the exclusion of alternatives is particularly true of the patterns of tax traditionally adopted by Hispanic states. Although now abandoned in its full extent by Spain and Portugal and pursued less rigorously by other states, several South American states (including, for example, Brasil and the Andean Pact states) still maintain that taxing competence is limited to those activities with their source within the state. This is possibly a reflection of the particularly strong sense of territorial sovereignty asserted within and by those states. It may be noted that an aspect of the source basis of taxation was subject to scrutiny and criticism by a panel of experts reviewing the French, Belgian and Dutch exemption-based systems in the context of the GATT. The panel found that the systems were not as such fully consistent with the limitations on those states under their GATT obligations, and these findings were adopted by the GATT authorities. They were to be explored further as part of the Uruguay Round, but so far it is understood little progress has been made.

518. The source basis also appears in those states, and in others attracted to this approach, in the methods of double tax relief granted. Those who base claims to tax on a source basis will if consistent exempt non-source income, that is, they will seek only to tax income sourced in the territory. Consequently income derived from elsewhere will not be taxed. In the usual jargon, it is exempted. By contrast, those relying on a personal approach to tax, or a residence basis, will have a potential claim over the worldwide income of the taxpayer. Relief here needs to be given by offset or credit against that worldwide charge.

The assertion of personal sovereignty

519. The territorial approach contrasts with an alternative approach, based on the personal sovereignty of a state. This approach, which derives its basis from tribal and feudal approaches to the structure of society and harks back to a time when states were more defined by personal loyalties than territorial boundaries, asserts the right to impose the laws of the sovereign on all those who 'belong' to the sovereign. A state is the modern personification of a sovereign (only in the UK can it be said that the sovereign, or Crown, is still 'the' state in a formal constitutional sense). As such, it is therefore entitled to assert its laws against its peoples regardless of what they are doing and where they are doing it. On this approach, territorial sovereignty need be asserted only against aliens.

520. The 'national' approach requires underpinning by a second set of rules, those which allocate persons to states. International public law provides some framework of rules for this allocation. They will not be explored here, because a recent book by Martha (*The Jurisdiction to Tax in International Law*, Kluwer, 1989) has done so fairly thoroughly. In practice, nationality is used as a basis for taxation of individuals by the United States of America and a only few other states (for example, the Philippines), and there has been little change to that attitude world-wide in the last 60 years or so. Again, nationality is not likely to be used widely in a positive sense as a basis of sales taxation because of the obvious advantage that would give foreigners.

Nationality and residence

521. This 'national' approach is sometimes regarded as being the counterpart in international public law terms to the 'source' approach, a counterpart referred to as the 'residence' approach. But identification of taxpayer to state is said to arise not when the taxpayer is a national of the state, but when the taxpayer is a resident of the state. That, as we argue below, is really an assertion of territorial jurisdiction, not personal jurisdiction. In a negative sense, the imposition of taxes on non-nationals but not on nationals may well be a tempting approach for internal political reasons, and a number of international arrangements and treaty-based approaches operate to try and curb it. Currently even in the negative form there is little practice of nationality based claims to tax individuals.

Claiming jurisdiction over legal persons

522. Nationality is increasingly asserted as a basis for jurisdiction for a state's direct taxes over legal persons. The state of nationality, in this sense, is taken as the state the laws of which give legal personality to a non-individual person, for example a company or a partnership. As Martha describes (in Section 9) this is a widely accepted rule of international law.

523. The UK made a significant change in its jurisdictional approach to taxation when, in 1988 and with little discussion, it shifted the basis of its taxation of companies largely on to an incorporation test. In so doing, it aligned its laws with the United States and many other common law countries and also with France, Germany and most other Community states (which use a siege social test but, as Martha also notes, define the siege social by national laws as determined or related to the state of incorporation). In trading terms, nationality is now the prevalent approach to asserting jurisdiction over such taxpayers although the term 'residence' is still widely used both internationally and in national laws. Justification for

a nationality based test is not often articulated, but one reason given by the United Kingdom for its change was that it wished to ensure that its company laws were not being abused.

524. This assertion of nationality-based jurisdiction reflects a shift in several major states during this century. The basic approach in English law (and therefore, at one time, throughout the British Empire) was to draw a direct analogy between companies and individuals. This was because the original law was silent on the issue. The approach to taxation of individuals was, historically, through the concept of 'residence' and accordingly this was applied to companies also. That approach has now been abandoned by most of the former Empire states, being replaced usually by a deeming approach. Thus in Britain, Canada, Australia, India, New Zealand and several developing states a company incorporated in the state is now deemed to be a resident of the state. The former English rule remains in the Republic of Ireland, Hong Kong, Singapore, the Channel Islands and a number of other states often regarded as low-tax territories.

525. What we see is a shift in the basis on which taxation is levied on artificial persons from a territorial basis to a personal basis. This coincides with a shift in practical forms of cross-border transaction. Increasingly, this is through the vehicle of artificial persons, rather than directly by individuals. Unlike the position in the UK, a partnership is an artificial person in many states and falls within these general comments. Most cross-border transactions now occur through entities over which states assert a personal taxing jurisdiction, in addition to any territorial claims. Is that shift important?

Claims over overseas corporations

526. Another, more recent, basis of claim over corporations is also emerging. This is the claim over foreign corporations controlled by corporations within the jurisdiction asserted by most of the major developed states, starting with the USA's provisions on Controlled Foreign Corporations (Subpart F), and adopted by Canada, Japan, the UK (following the Japanese example), Germany, and, from 1990, Australia. The assertion of jurisdiction is aimed at 'tax haven' companies, but it cannot derive its legal validity from that basis.

527. Stripped of the anti-avoidance aspects, the assertion is that a taxpayer within the jurisdiction can be made taxable on the profits of a subsidiary corporation outside the jurisdiction. This is not a territorial claim in the sense of 'source state' – rather, the exact reverse. Nor is it a territorial claim on the basis of residence. It is essentially a further claim on the basis

of nationality on the implicit basis that a subsidiary company is the property of the controlling shareholder. Whilst this is a recognition of economic reality, it runs against the well-established rule of international public law whereby the shareholders of a company have no competence to take up the case of that company in international public law through their (the shareholders') government against the company's government.

528. Alternatively, the claim is based on the protective principle: that a state has jurisdiction over persons and activities which have a direct effect on its economy or nationals. The latter claim is one asserted by states in a different context to justify commando raids into other states' territories or preemptive strikes, and is clearly more controversial than a claim based on nationality.

529. By contrast, one attempt to assert jurisdiction over a corporation solely on the basis of residence met strong protests – the claim to unitary taxation of corporate profits. Several states of the USA asserted some years ago a claim over a 'proper' share of the total worldwide profits of multinational companies on the basis that they were, through subsidiaries, resident (because economically active) in the territory of the state. Again, the method of apportioning world-wide profits is irrelevant to the legal jurisdictional claim. Many states, including the United States Federal Government, refuted this claim, although not on express grounds of an absence of jurisdictional competence.

530. This may be because, in Martha's words, 'absent any rule in general international law that prohibits [a state] from employing the unitary method . . . no jurisdictional argument can be legally invoked against [it] . . . Guidelines will not suffice.' It is not enough, as some have suggested it is, that there is a general understanding between states about the way treaties should deal with this issue. Martha argues, as do others, that unitary taxation may be in breach of other rules of international general law, but they are not relevant here. In effect, the point about general understanding is supported by the fact that most of the taxing authorities previously using or interested in using this basis have now desisted from so doing. One may note that, a little ironically, if the remaining US states do abandon this basis for claiming jurisdiction, the general principle of law argued for may have then emerged. But we are not at that position yet.

531. One conclusion from these various developments is that, in handling the affairs of a multinational, residence of a subsidiary is not a satisfactory basis to tax the parent where it is itself not within the taxing jurisdiction, but ownership of a subsidiary is a sufficient basis to tax the parent on the profits of the subsidiary. If that is so, it strengthens the shift towards a per-

·itorial assertion of jurisdiction on companies. A sec-
be that neither development evidences clear think-
ıal limits of jurisdiction of international public law,
:s, a mixture of economic and political realities.

er individuals

sertion of direct tax jurisdiction over individuals
t, based on 'residence' (so termed both interna-
eaking states; 'domicile' is a prevalent internal
ıere is no one approach to defining 'residence',
ır statutory or administrative definitions have
One theme within those definitions is that
define residence. Why?

recently explored the derivation of this con-
Their discussions and the results of their
; the new patterns took full account of the
· beyond the scope of this work except to
proach to 'residence' predates both the
ıeir modern form and, equally, the mod-
ational public law. Rather less obviously
ın of nationality in the UK and was, in
ıther than *personal* jurisdiction. This is
of individuals with the Kingdom was
giance', itself operated as a territorial
f personal assertion of laws that was
ctuating frontiers, as in continental

many developed states make this
; a modern tendency to define pre-
ax purposes. Common factors in
ividual has a permanent home or
's employment is located; where
days a year test recurring regu-

ırea of direct tax in most states
ıent will be the source of the
:he location of the employee.
rce test. This breaks down in
ıd', and special rules are fre-
;. One answer is to recogni-

se only the taxing competence of the 'usual' state of the employee, cially if the employment abroad is brief.

536. Another is to pursue the 'source' approach, and tax the emplo where it is. The two bases are recognised as alternatives for direct t poses, but this divided claim cannot subsist so easily for social s contribution purposes, and one answer must prevail. That answe location of employment, the use of which is central to thinking i security taxes. These taxes have tended to take their conceptu from the employment laws along with which they operate, thus u conflicts laws from employment law to solve the locational ques tax liability. This has arisen through the activities of the Inte Social Security Association, a body linked to the Internationa Organisation.

Source, residence or nationality?

537. Given the confusion of possible jurisdictional answers, th of major problems of double taxation is not surprising. The suggests, however, that shifts are occurring and may potenti occur in the overall answer without much specific attention be to those shifts. Essentially, the jurisdiction to tax has been c territorial basis though as a matter of past practicalities rath theory. More recently, as we have seen, nationality has be basis for taxing artificial persons but this has not developed taxing individuals.

538. The territorial claim comes in two forms: that of the item being taxed – its source, and that of the person being t dence. For internal indirect taxes, which by definition are l not persons, there is little choice and the source basis (in is, of the source of the money used to pay the tax) is used essence of the tax. Where international transactions are ca has existed (as with VAT), the source basis has also pre reason being that the tax in its common form is consumer

539. In direct taxation rivalry has long existed as betwee and a residence basis. This has been the central dilemma ing to secure agreement to model double taxation conv out this century and, as we noted above, the models fr double competence to tax. Nonetheless, the prevailing 1977 OECD model is that of the underlying world-wi the state of residence, with the later UN model depart number of specific provisions to favour more the state thinking in resolving this dispute is noted later.

2 RECENT CHANGES IN TAX TECHNIQUES

540. Two kinds of change have been occurring, as indicated above. The first is in the underlying basis of claim to tax, with the assertion on a general basis of a personal claim over corporations (though the change has been obscured by the use of the same terminology of 'residence' for a nationality based claim as a territorially based claim). The second is in the balance between the assertion of the residence/origin states' claims as against the source/destination states' claims.

541. The first of the shifts is a disguised shift from the residence basis of tax. As noted, this is obscured semantically because it is still called the residence basis. Nonetheless a claim on the basis on nationality is regardless of the residence of the company in the sense of the location of its management (either central or day-to-day). It is not, however, a shift towards source state taxation, but rather the general assertion of a third variable.

542. The second of the shifts arises from the general reforms of taxation noted earlier in this study. There arc several different reasons why there is a shift from state of residence to state of source resulting from those reforms:

(a) the shift towards *social security taxes* involves the acceptance of the primacy in most states of the location of employment over the residence of the employee as the basis of tax. This is subject to variation in individual or regional agreements, and an exception of 6 months, a year or, sometimes, 2 or 3 years, is widely used during which the state of permanent residence maintains its claim over someone temporarily overseas. These periods are tending to shorten towards a maximum of one year. They are, however, strictly exceptions. The clear consensus view is that an employee cannot be compelled to be insured under more than one social security system. It follows that the assertion of the location of employment is one which excludes any taxation by the state of residence.

(b) Shifts within *indirect taxation* have confirmed the predominance of source/destination state competence. This is because of the form of VAT widely adopted, often in place of sales taxes. Insofar as VAT is replacing manufacturing taxes (as in Canada) or excises levied at an early stage in the production process (as in some EC states) there is a shift towards the source/destination state from the residence/origin state. Import taxes, now of lesser importance, are source state taxes, so the picture is not uniform. Further, if the EC shifts to an origin-based VAT, this will of itself make a significant reversal of current trends.

(c) any *shift from direct to indirect tax* will probably result in a shift towards source state taxation. The precise picture will vary from state to state, but where a state such as the UK has a strong preference for the residence basis of direct tax, and reduces that by transferring the budgetary burden to indirect taxes like VAT, it does so by replacing the residence based income taxes with source based VAT.

(d) Shifts towards *local taxation* may result in shifts towards source based taxation. This will depend on the forms of local taxation used, and their jurisdictional rules. If, as in West Germany, the local taxes in part are parallel to the national taxes, no shift will occur. But if, as in Japan or the UK, there is a strong element of land and property taxation in the local taxes, the shift will occur as it will if, as in the USA, local taxes are strongly of the indirect variety.

(e) Any *shift from taxes to charges* will tend to prevent any form of double taxation relief arising. Insofar as it does, it will increase source state levies as regards a residence based claim to tax at the level of tax. Against that, the charge can presumably be regarded as a deductible expense in the residence state, thereby offsetting the loss of double tax relief to some extent.

(f) The shifts within *corporate taxes* have been, as noted above, partly based by a shift to a nationality base for tax which is independent of source or residence. Insofar as the previous basis was usually residence (as in those states following the former English approach) there has again been a shift away from the residence basis. The move towards *economic integration of corporation and shareholder* will, depending on the precise treatment under DTAs, suggest a shift towards source based taxes. This is pursued further below. So also is the question of the effect of the flattening of the range of *corporate tax rates,* which tends to make any withholding tax more important. As it does so (as with dividends and interest) so it again makes the claim of the source state more economically significant. By contrast, the moves to widen the tax base, especially in relation to overseas activities of corporations, detracts from the source based approach, and increase the potential collection by the state of nationality.

(g) The extent of *anti-avoidance* measures will have mixed effects. Controlled foreign company legislation captures tax from a subsidiary foreign source to the state of the parent company's nationality. Transfer pricing can operate to the advantage of source, residence or nationality; challenges to debt-equity ratios and similar provisions tend to benefit the state of the subsidiary source of the parent company's income.

(h) Playing down the importance of *personal direct taxes* means that taxpayers most likely to be subjected to double taxation are now taxed at lower marginal rates in many developed states.
Again, this will emphasise the importance of any withholding tax or tax levied in the source state (for example, on employment there). However, moves to widen the tax base, especially as regards measures with foreign elements, will emphasise the residence approach.

543. The above series of points strongly suggest that in general there is a swing towards an emerging dominance of source/destination-based tax competence as against residence/origin-based competence, in other words, the place where the activity occurs rather than the person is located, but with emerging personal-based competence for corporate taxpayers and group profits. These are, of course, conflicting trends, and suggest a growth of economic double taxation even if the direct formal double taxation within the framework of similar taxes is not so marked.

3 GRANTING DOUBLE TAX RELIEF

544. We started this chapter by challenging the assumption that treaties for double tax relief were designed to secure relief for the taxpayer. Yet in the last chapter we noted the growing reliance on treaty-based solutions to double taxation. We must now explore how treaties have been dealing with double taxation, and how the recent shifts in taxation patterns have themselves altered the answers to the problems of double taxation.

The growth of bilateral treaties

545. One undoubted trend of recent years in international taxation has the clear pattern of adoption of solutions to double tax problems through bilateral agreements. Furthermore, those treaties have, in their form, equally undoubtedly been strongly influenced by the model conventions adopted by the OECD (and on which the other models of the UN and USA have been closely based). As Phillips chronicles (in J S Phillips, Tax Treaty Networks, 1989, Worldwide Information), the relationships of the eleven major trading nations are dominated inter se by this form of agreement.

546. The only 'missing' treaties from the 55 possibilities (between Australia, Brasil, Canada, France, Italy, Japan, Netherlands, Switzerland, UK, USA, Germany) are between Brasil and Australia, Netherlands, Switzerland, the UK and the USA. Recent economic changes in Brasil may lead to even these gaps being removed. But Phillips observes 'the actual network of bilateral treaties [between the eleven states]

involves numerous variations between one treaty and another', as his work details.

Reasons for double tax agreements

547. Before examining whether the terms of individual agreements differ radically from the models, it is worth considering why agreements are arrived at between states.

548. If tax relief against double tax is intended, then those states whose taxpayers suffer excess tax can secure relief by only three techniques, absent an alignment of tax competences. The first two are by international agreement, multilateral or bilateral, the third is by unilateral or national measures.

549. During the last two decades a number of attempts have been made, as noted in the last chapter, to secure multilateral relief. Nearly all failed, and none are currently likely to appear in the near future. Indeed, one set (those of COMECON) will disappear. These is too little consistency either of tax structure or tax competence to make this approach readily feasible.

550. The unilateral approach is also not popular. This is because this kind of relief requires a state to surrender a good deal of national revenue whilst securing nothing in return for the state or its taxpayers. In the absence of some external limits, the reduction of tax by one state may simply increase the tax levied by another state benefitting only the taxpayers of that other state. Paradoxically, therefore, the taxpayers for whom the relief was introduced may end up worse off.

551. The bilateral vehicle to double tax relief is therefore the only method likely to achieve success between systems as disparate as those operating at present. But, what is 'success'? Is it achievement of taxpayer neutrality, or are other reasons behind the widespread adoption of double tax agreements?

552. Adoption of double tax agreements was slow prior to the late 1940s, and developed rapidly only in the last 25 years. The reasons behind the UK's adoption of DTAs is instructive in noting this pattern. Previously, the UK had undertaken some measures to alleviate the burden of double taxation within the Empire. In 1916 relief was granted to those who had paid both UK and 'Colonial' tax. The taxpayer would pay a reduced rate of UK tax, but this would not be less than 17.5%. In 1919 a Royal Commission looked into the problem and as a result a system of 'Dominion

Income Tax Relief' was implemented in 1920. This resulted in relief of up to half the UK rate for the double taxation of income and profits within the Empire. It applied to non-residents and was a unilateral relief measure (although it was hoped that the other party would make up the difference which was in fact what happened on most occasions).

553. Between the wars no double taxation agreements were signed apart from an agreement with Ireland based solely on the residence principle. Towards the end of the second world war, the United States approached the UK on the possibility of negotiating a double taxation agreement and in 1945 the UK signed its first comprehensive double taxation agreement.

554. After signing its first comprehensive treaty relatively late, the UK's treaty network grew very rapidly over the next five years when thirty comprehensive double taxation agreements were negotiated, almost exclusively with the then colonies. The fiscal reasons for this have already been mentioned, although what may have largely been overlooked are the non-fiscal, primarily political reasons for this change of approach and the new desire to negotiate and conclude double taxation agreements with states (colonies) with whom trading links at the time were minimal. Since we could find no material (governmental and non-governmental) to explain why this shift in policy had occurred, we decided to search for the answer at source, through the Public Records Library.

Non-tax reasons for tax agreements

555. Although quite a number of files remain closed beyond the 30 year period generally applicable in the UK for public documents, from the files to which we were allowed access it became apparent that non-fiscal reasons played a major part, if not the major part in the UK's new involvement in the tax treaty network.

556. File IR 40/ 12093 consists mainly of intra-governmental communication between the Treasury, the Foreign Office and the Inland Revenue on possible agreements. At an early stage in the change of view (March 1945), a letter from the Board of Trade argued, about DTAs with China and Egypt:

'Both these countries are . . . . important for our foreign trade, and in both of them it is important to get the best safeguards we can for our people and our companies – particularly because both in China and in Egypt they have until recently enjoyed the protection of regimes of extraterritoriality which have now disappeared. Moreover in both of these countries we have to look for a wave of nationalist and anti-foreign feeling which, in the absence of treaty safeguards, may work serious harm to British interests operating there.'

557. Later that year, the Foreign Office also noted, in accepting these views:
'We are however anxious to guard against our people in China being subjected to irregular taxation levied by provincial authorities, that is to say taxation levied in accordance with rules and regulations issued by the provincial authorities at their own will and pleasure. Our experience in China justifies our taking special precautions in this respect.'

558. The reference to exterritoriality reminds of a system now largely forgotten in its then extant form whereby foreigners (usually Europeans) within a state (usually in what is now the third world) were granted immunity from local laws, and remained subject only to their national laws. At one time this was a common approach to solving conflicts of laws problems, but the growth of the 'absolute' sovereign state along with the ending of the colonial phase of development has rendered this approach largely inappropriate. For tax purposes the modern equivalents of this are free zones and freeports or the sovereign base areas such as that of the UK in Cyprus. The system of exterritoriality was one based on the nationality of individuals and, as we have seen, has now been dropped as an approach to taxation jurisdiction by most states.

559. Other papers in the file emphasize the political reasons for the negotiation of double taxation agreements. One of the main reasons seems to be that after the Second World War relations with foreign powers needed to be settled and because nationalist feelings were running high some sort of protection (mainly from discrimination) was required of the interests of UK subjects.

560. A few years later, the subject of the British approach to double taxation agreements received its only public scrutiny, as part of the proceedings of the Royal Commission on the Taxation of Profits and Income. During the Commission's considerations, comments were invited about double taxation. In response, the Westminster Chamber of Commerce, amongst others, made a submission. It recommended unilateral 100 per cent double taxation relief in all cases.

561. In rejecting this approach, a joint Treasury and Inland Revenue reply (filed at IR40 / 10994) stated:

> . . . A uniform code of Double Taxation Relief which would satisfy the Westminster Chamber of Commerce could not be anything

short of 100% unilateral relief, which we have hitherto rejected for various reasons.

In 1950 we decided that we could not give 100% relief because if we did, we should give up a bargaining counter which is useful to us in our efforts to conclude bilateral Tax Relief Agreements. Up to the present, we have not changed our views and we still hope to conclude further bilateral agreements.

We could not amend our existing agreements unilaterally as the Westminster Chamber of Commerce appear to desire, nor would we wish to.

The advantages of the bilateral agreement systems are firstly that for some forms of income such as non – Government pensions, interest, patent and copyright royalties and shipping and air transport profits, the country of origin of the income normally bears the burden of relief. 100% unilateral relief would therefore be more costly to the Exchequer because under the agreements, the burden of relief is shared in this way.

Secondly, we are able by means of extra agreements to get other tax authorities to agree to employ desirable principles of taxation and to apply certain limits to the taxation of our enterprises, for example, agreement not to levy discriminatory taxation on our nationals and to limit tax on our enterprises to only those profits derived from the other country through a permanent establishment.

Thirdly, the agreements provide for the exchange of information between the tax authorities and so help in the prevention of evasion.

If we were to give 100% unilateral relief, we should reduce the chances of concluding bilateral Agreements because the other countries would point out that we already gave full relief for foreign tax and would say that they saw no necessity to share the burden. In addition, if we now gave 100% unilateral relief, those countries with which we already have Agreements might feel that they were bearing a part of our burden of relief unnecessarily.
Unilateral relief of up to 50% of the rate of tax in the case of purely foreign tax, and up to 75% in the case of Commonwealth tax, does in any case substantially relieve the greater part of foreign tax not covered by Agreements.

The agreements involve two parties each of whom protects his own taxpayers as far as possible, whether in relation to securing concessions from the other or retaining the right to tax income in the other country. A uniform pattern of agreement forms the basis of the discussions preliminary to signature and agreed variations are written in. It is, however, clearly impossible to impose a standard form of agreement on other countries or to expect the adoption of such an agreement by all other countries, whatever their financial and other relations with the U.K., the way in which income flows between the two countries or the fiscal system of the other country. If the other country insists on retaining a particular form of taxation as in the case of insurance by Australia, Ceylon and New Zealand, the alternative to acceptance of the condition is the failure to complete an agreement.

The provisions for unilateral relief were an important advance in the scheme of relief and it would be undesirable to widen the scope of the allowance for tax imposed in countries with which double taxation agreements have not yet been made so long as there is a prospect of a full agreement being made.

562. More recent thinking in the United Kingdom, as related to specific double taxation agreements, is not usually a matter of public record. The general view is that, whatever the specific aims in individual cases, and aside from the interest in revenue sharing and reduction of double taxation, there is an advantage in a double taxation agreement simply because it is there. In other words, the certainty of the terms under which the two tax authorities will handle bilateral flows is of itself an advantage.

563. This contrasts with the procedures in some other states, especially the United States. There, all treaties (including the US-UK agreements) have been subject to public scrutiny, and Congressional records form an important source of thinking on these treaties – which are not as extensive as those of Western European states. This may be partly because the Senate has attempted to alter a number of draft treaties to such an extent that the potential other party has refused to accept the version approved by the Senate.

Recent US tax treaty policy

564. An authoritative article by Reese in 1987 surveys the reasoning behind US DTAs and previous literature. It focusses particularly on the agreement with China which took effect in 1986. In doing so it reviews policy objectives.

Reese identifies four areas of tax policy objective:

- preventing double taxation
- preventing tax avoidance and evasion
- reducing barriers to trade and investment
- special developing country concerns.

He also identifies classes of both economic and political foreign policy objective.

565. Reese notes the standpoint of the USA on worldwide tax competence based on a residence claim, but notes how in the China treaty (as in the Jamaica treaty concluded in 1980) the USA concede source-based taxation ' to an unprecedented extent, in some provisions going even beyond the UN Model approach.' it was said on the Congressional record that this was in exchange for substantial concessions by the treaty partners, but Reese comments that these concessions were not identified '. . . and are not obvious from the text of the treaty, which departs from the US Model, it seems, only to China's benefit.' The conclusion is that political concerns dominated economic concerns, and specifically tax concerns, in the conclusion of the China treaty as others, and that this is evidence that the United States is prone to entering overly generous and overly politicised agreements.

566. The above examples serve to show the danger of reading only taxation implications from DTAs. In noting the extent to which the OECD or UN models have been adopted, we must also accept the proviso that political explanations extraneous to taxation may be the reasons for particular developments.

Recent practice in the adoption and operation of treaty terms

567. Two topics arise for present discussion: first, have recent tax reforms affected the operation of the model, and of treaties following that form? Second, how far has that form in fact been used by states? All details of wording that differ from the model are obviously important, but are these differences to adjust the general concepts to individual systems, or do they reflect non-acceptance of the general model? In particular, in the present context, has there been any shifting in attitudes?

568. It must be stated, by way of preface to this discussion, that there has been little systematic study of the variations in treaties from a conceptual standpoint. The work by Phillips is the first sustained analysis of differences between texts. Analysis is also made possible by compendiums of treaties such as that now put on CD ROM by the International Bureau for Fiscal Documentation. National studies have also appeared, starting with

those emanating from the United States. But, aside from the work of Edwardes-Ker, there has been little analysis of practice behind the texts, let alone comparative conceptual analysis.
The present study is therefore, unfortunately, anecdotal rather than systematic as the required analysis was beyond our resources.

Operation of the models in the light of recent reforms

(a) *definition articles*

569. The first point of importance to note arises with Article 2, the taxes covered by the model. Insofar as there is a definite trend to rely less on direct taxes, so the coverage of the model is diminished. It does not cover social security taxes (nor, outside the USA, does anyone appear to have argued that it should, notwithstanding the imbalanced position that emerges in dealing with Australia, for example). It does not cover local taxation other than income and capital taxation (and many individual double taxation conventions do not even go as far as the model on this). It does not cover, nor purport to cover, any form of indirect tax – and individual treaties covering both direct and indirect tax do not, it is believed, exist anywhere.

570. The next article affected is the definition of 'resident'. This is because as states adopt nationality as a basis for corporate direct taxation, so the wording of Article 4.1 is put under some pressure, as is the rule on dual residence of companies in Article 4.3, and the commentary statement that 'it would not be an adequate solution to attach importance to a purely formal criterion like registration'. It is suggested that current practice evidences a shift of international thinking on that point.

571. The example of the US-UK agreement, in omitting all mention of dual resident companies, whilst now out of date in that particular context, seems more understandable internationally. This is consistent with the general US position which is stated by way of reservation to the OECD commentary, as is that of Canada. Provisions such as this in a number of other UK treaties may now be regarded as potentially out-of-date and presumably subject to review on an appropriate future occasion. The Canada-Italy treaty deems such a company not to be a resident of either state (which has broadly the same effect).

572. The Brasil-Canada treaty leaves the question to bilateral discussion, as does the Canada-UK agreement, and several Japanese agreements. This is consistent with the dissent by Japan to the OECD commentary.

573. By contrast the Australia-Canada, Canada-Switzerland agreements give priority to the state of registration, in contradiction to the model commentary. The Italy West Germany agreement relies on the registered office as does the Dutch-Swiss agreement, which will broadly have the same effect.

574. Although brief, this survey suggests the major dissent to the 1977 model by the USA and Japan (and also Canada) has been compounded by more recent developments and by individual treaties.

575. The final definition in the first part of the model is that of permanent establishment. Although vitally important to the structure of the model, and subject to individual differences dealing, for example, with oil rigs and insurance companies, this article seems to have reached broad acceptance except, perhaps, to the building site rule (twelve months required) in article 5.3. The UN model set, instead, a six months rule. Recent treaties have quite often adopted this (eg India's treaties) or a nine month rule (as in the German-Kuwait and Czechoslovakia-Greece agreements). Insofar as variants appear elsewhere, they are in favour of widening the definition, and therefore of reflecting a shift to source based taxation, as does the reduction in the duration of a building site before it is relevant.

(b) *articles on the taxation of income*

576. Turning to the longest and most important part of the treaty – articles 6 to 21 on the division of competence for differing forms of income – three general observations can be made.

577. The first is that the pattern of modern bilateral treaties almost invariably accepts the breakdown and broad approach of these articles, as does the UN model, which means that the OECD model significantly sets and shapes international double taxation rules on these topics. As older treaties are renegotiated, so this dominance extends. The dominance does not remove, as it cannot, underlying differences such as that between immoveable property and real property (or realty) which prevents article 6 being adopted unamended as widely as might otherwise be the case.
It follows that conceptual distinctions such as that between dividends and other distributions on the one part and interest and debt-service payments on the other part form the basis of all such agreements. Issues of reclassification (as in cases of thin capitalisation) tend in part to be viewed as problematic because of this schematic approach.

578. A second comment is that, both here and elsewhere, several major states are now insisting on insertion and strengthening of anti-abuse pro-

visions to deal with profit-shifting and treaty shopping practices. This appears chiefly in the OECD 1977 model in the form of article 9. Paragraph 2 of article 9 (on transfer pricing adjustments) met major resistance in 1977, with seven states dissenting from it, and the US arguing about its scope. Treaties negotiated before and at that time often omitted it, as, for example, have the major Japanese treaties.

579. In the last few years attitudes in Japan and elsewhere have changed, sometimes quite sharply, on issues such as transfer pricing. In part, it is suggested, this is a direct reflection of the pressures on states to broaden their direct tax bases. As they have done so, so the need has arisen to deal with tax avoidance under bilateral treaties – both in preventing the use of treaties for avoidance purposes and strengthening treaty provisions to tackle avoidance. At the extreme this has meant the abrogation of treaties, such as those with the Netherlands Antilles. It has also led to treaty override provisions in national law commented on in the previous chapter, the most significant measure of which (the US branch profits tax) has itself started to appear in bilateral treaties (as with the recent USA-Spain agreement) by way of specific provision.

580. This changing attitude to the extent to which treaties deal with abuse has also been supported by the toughening of attitudes by a number of leading tax authorities (for example the US, UK, German, French and Dutch) to such issues both in their rulings and their handling of individual matters. This again reflects the need to broaden the tax base of direct taxes in order to sustain lower overall rates.

581. The third general comment again reflects the patterns of recent tax reform internationally. A major change is the reduction of the marginal rates of tax applied to both individual and corporate direct taxes. Where only one state has taxing competence, that is a matter of national significance alone. But where taxing competence is shared, the international impact is frequently significant.

582. Shared competence is provided for by the model for business profits of permanent establishments and fixed bases in the other state, employment abroad, and, by way of withholding taxes, for dividends, interest and (in the UN model) royalties. In other words, it is the general position. To that, one recent note of dissent should be added. This is the resolve of the European Commission to remove source-based taxation of income flows from subsidiaries to parent companies, a resolve now starting to find legal form. However, this has, at the time of writing, only just started to emerge from the shadow land of ideas it occupied for over two decades.

583. Taken together, these aspects of direct taxation cover all transfers of capital income and of earnings sourced in one state but remitted to the other, aside from aspects of real property taxation. The emerging rate patterns for both income taxes and corporate profits taxes have a two-fold effect on the operation of treaties following the OECD model.

(c) *A shift to source-based taxation*

584. One is that, as rates converge (as it is argued that, at least superficially, corporate tax rates are doing), so the scope for a second 'slice' of taxation by the state of residence, after full taxation by the source state, is reduced and may disappear. For example, a source state levies tax on profits earned from professional services performed in that state by an individual resident in another state. The source state will probably levy tax at the basic or main rate of income tax, or at any rate at a rate below the maximum. Some years ago this may have been at, say, 30 per cent. The individual would be taxed in his state of residence on a strongly progressive scale of rates, and might have a marginal tax rate of, say, 75 per cent. He would therefore, in many states, pay 30 per cent to the source state and 45 per cent to the residence state.

585. The same person might now be paying perhaps 20 or 25 per cent to the source state on similar income, but would typically face much lower marginal rates in his state of residence, say 40 per cent to 50 per cent, so paying perhaps 25 per cent to each of the two states. This illustrates the fact that, typically, the gap between the main rates of income tax (the rates payable on average levels of income) and the top marginal rates are much lower than they were, a reduction greater in proportion than the reductions in main rates of tax. In such cases, therefore, there is an effective shift in tax shares towards the source state and away from the residence state.

586. Arguably much more important than this practical effect in favour of a source state is the conceptual consequence of the change of tax structure this illustrates. One reason commonly cited as justifying the residence-based approach to direct taxation of individuals is that otherwise the tax system fails to be progressive. Unless one could cumulate in at least one state, the argument runs, the total world-wide income of an individual, and tax it in that state on a progressive scale, the system would be unfair as against those with only one national source of income.

587. Whilst that argument may have been a strong one before present reforms, its strength is much diminished now. Indeed, it is of hardly any relevance at all for some states such as the UK where the marginal rate of tax is now relatively low, and of no importance to states which adopt a flat

rate income tax structure. It is, one might also note here, largely irrelevant as a justification for residence-based taxation of corporations.

(d) *Withholding taxes*

588. The other effect of the new rate structure is upon withholding taxes. These have become more significant as a result of cuts in other rates, whilst the model rates – and rates in individual treaties – have not been changed. For example, the dividend article (article 10) provided for withholding rates of 5 and 15 per cent at a time when many main corporate rates were over 50 per cent, and when individual top marginal rates were of the order of 75 per cent or more. Thus, typically, under the classical system of corporation tax the source state would be taking 5 per cent of a total tax take of over 50 per cent, and 15 per cent of a total tax take of perhaps 75 per cent.

589. Under typical modern rate structures, and without a change of withholding, the source state might be taking 5 per cent of a total tax take of 35 to 40 per cent, and 15 per cent of a total tax take of 40 to 50 per cent. Here again we see a further significant shift to source state taxation.

590. Where imputation systems or other offsetting systems are operating, and a view is taken of the combined effect of both the tax charge on the profits and on the dividend paid from them, the picture is a little more complicated. Take for example the UK system, and a typical double tax treaty allowing credit, but imposing the 15 per cent withholding. The pattern on a distributable profit totalling £100 is:

'Old' system		'New' system	
Distribution	100	Distribution	100
CT at 52%	52	CT at 35%	35
Distributable profit	48	Distributable profit	65
Add back ACT (35/65)	26	Add back ACT (1/3)	22
Gross dividend	74	Gross dividend	87
Withholding at 15%	11	Withholding at 15%	13
net dividend received	63	net dividend received	74
Residence state tax (say 52% less DTR on 74)	27	Residence state tax (say 35% less DTR on 87)	17
Shareholder receives	36	Shareholder receives	57
Source state receives	37	Source state receives	26
Residence state receives	27	Residence state receives	17

591. Under this example, source state tax is diminished by 17 per cent on the direct charge, but the ACT adjustment is also reduced and the take from the withholding increases by 2 per cent, so making the effective tax reduction only 11 per cent. The residence state rate also nominally diminishes by 17 per cent. The effective tax take drops from 27 per cent to 17 per cent, a drop of much less, because the residence state rate is applied in this example to the post-source-state-tax profit from the company.

592. This example suggests that for the growing number of states with imputation systems of corporation tax, or other forms of partial or total offset, comments based only on the OECD model may be misleading. Even so, on our above example we see the shift towards source state taxation is operative on the rates structures chosen. Under the old system, the source state keeps 37 of the total tax of 64 collected, whilst under the new system it is 26 of the total of 43, an increase of over 2 per cent in the total share of tax going to the source state.

593. The OECD model recommended a withholding of 10 per cent on interest payment. As with the classical system of dividend taxation, the withholding will here be of markedly greater significance against a background rate of tax reduced in most states for both corporate and individual recipients.

594. Finally, the OECD model recommends no withholding on royalties, whilst the UN model does recommend withholdings. They are quite common, even occurring between OECD states and, perhaps a little more surprisingly, between EEC members (all of whom are also OECD members). A typical rate of withholding might be 10 per cent. Again, this will have a heightened effect.

595. It should be noted that, aside from German tax treaties, few DTAs have provisions which adjust the withholding relative to the underlying main rates. The Germans, having announced major alterations to their tax rates, are negating this automatic change by seeking renegotiations of their treaties.

596. The above arguments strongly suggest that withholding tax rates ought to be reduced in line with the overall reductions in tax – from 15 per cent to perhaps 12 or 10 per cent, and from 5 per cent to 3 per cent (if such a tax is still worth collecting).

597. There is some evidence that such cuts are starting to work through into recent agreements amongst the most developed states. The five-state Nordic multilateral convention has recently been renegotiated to reduce

withholding taxes on dividends, as have the very important German-US agreement, and the France-Italy and Germany-Italy agreements. (The reduction is not universal, however, as withholdings are imposed or increased on profit participating loans and real estate investment trusts). The new US-Spain agreement opts for the OECD set withholdings, plus a 10 per cent royalties withholding in some cases, but this replaces previous withholding rates of 20 per cent (Spain) and 30 per cent (USA). The Canada-Luxembourg agreement leaves interest withholding at 15% and royalties withholding at 10%, with dividend withholding at between 5% and 15%, down (in the case of Canada) from 25%. The 1990 Netherlands-Norway agreement removes withholdings on dividends where there is a direct participation of 25%, but maintains withholdings on other dividends. The previous agreement had dispensed with withholdings on interest and royalties.

598. The final, but most important, example is the agreement within the member states of the European Community to cut withholdings on flows of dividends from subsidiary to parent by 1992 in the case of most states, and 1996 in the case of the laggards. Further, it is currently proposed to extend the same treatment within the corporate group to interest and royalty payments.Given that a significant share of all flows takes place intragroup, and that the Community rules are likely in due course to spread to other agreements, this may represent the start of an important new trend.

599. But by contrast, the new UK-Belgium agreement leaves interest withholding rates at 15% and increases the source state withholdings in some cases for dividends. It is interesting to note that shortly after concluding this treaty, the Belgian government had a change of heart, and proposed reduction of its main withholding rate on interest from securities, bonds and savings accounts from 25% to 10% as from March 1990 – which will presumably have effect for the treaty as well. The reason for this change was capital flight from Belgium, one may presume in large part to Luxembourg.

5000. Another potentially significant change of heart occurred in 1990 when the European Commission, having failed to attract support – despite strong lobbying and some national support – for its proposal for a Community-wide interest withholding of 15% then 10% completely altered its stance and came out, instead, for a long term objective of the abolition within the Community of all interest and royalty withholdings.

5001. Most recently, a powerful argument against withholdings has been presented by the Institute for Fiscal Studies in the UK (IFS Report No 35, Corporation Tax Harmonisation in the EC, 1989).

This suggests that withholding taxes on dividends are the single biggest barrier in corporation taxation to freeing flows of corporate money within the Single European Market, and far more significant than other tax differences. If that argument is accepted, it will be all the more unfortunate if one effect of reducing overall corporate tax rates is, paradoxically, to create bigger barriers to cross-border flows because of a reluctance to reduce withholdings in line with overall rates.

5002. It would seem that recent agreements outside the EEC and Group of 7 are using the OECD or UN recommended rates of withholding, including in a number of cases royalties withholdings. One example is the withholdings within recent Malaysian agreements, imposing 15% on both interest and royalties.

5003. This leads to mention of another area of concern in connection, in particular, with variable withholding rates, namely the third state problem. Typically, this arises where a resident of one state uses a branch or subsidiary in a second state in order to trade into or invest in a third state. This arises as a problem simply because there is no multilateral framework to ensure that the terms of trade and tax are neutral to indirect trading between the first and third state, rather than direct trading. Frequently such indirect trading proves advantageous, for example because of lower overall tax costs due to lower withholdings. This is seen by treaty parties as an abuse of the bilateral relationship. If so, it may be combatted by provisions requiring beneficial ownership within the two treaty parties, and not a third state. But this may lead to the reverse problem, namely that a company based in the first state cannot claim treaty relief through its base or subsidiary in the second state to the third state, even though it could have claimed similar relief if it had traded direct, because of restrictions in the relevant treaties. This problem exists in large part because of differential levels of withholding, and becomes worse if the withholdings become more significant.

(e) *Interaction of direct and indirect taxes*

5004. A final point may be made on cross-border capital income flows. Interest charges and similar payments are, in value added tax terms, payments for services. They are therefore potentially within the scope of the tax. In the EC model of the tax – and the pattern adopted in many other states – no tax is levied on interest or on other credit costs. This is because supplies of credit are exempted under the EC Sixth VAT Directive. However, the Directive gives governments the right to allow taxpayers to opt to tax such transactions. It is believed that all member states currently exempt banking and financial transactions with only Germany allowing the option to tax. Consideration in the USA of VAT has included a proposal to charge VAT on at least the element of interest which is a charge or intermediation services. This was also proposed originally by the Canadians for the Goods and Services Tax, but the proposal was later withdrawn.

5005. Were banking and financial services to cease to be exempted, an interesting position would arise in terms of the interaction with withholding taxes, because, in effect, VAT could impose a further withholding tax. Say that interest is being paid at 10 per cent on a loan of #10,000. Currently, that means that interest of #1,000 is payable. If a 10 per cent withholding, say, is operating on payment of that interest to another state, the source state will receive #100, and the lender #900. If VAT is imposed on the interest (rather than merely on the intermediation services), then on a supply of interest within one state, the interest would go up to reflect the VAT. Take a typical standard rate of VAT of 15 per cent. Then the interest payable will be #1,150.

5006. Under current rules, if the interest is payable cross-border, the loan would be a supply of international services exempted from tax in the state of origin and taxable (by way of a reverse charge or self-supply procedure) in the destination state (or, in income tax terms, the source state from which the interest is paid). This would indirectly operate as a withholding.

5007. Again surmising, were the VAT to be altered, as has been argued strongly, to an origin basis, a VAT charge on credit would become instead an origin state, or residence state, levy. Alternatively, it could be argued that such a series of changes could be used to get rid of the withholding taxes altogether, with limited budgetary loss to the source state. This series of assumptions shows how far the interaction of VAT with income tax could run if the process of widening the bases of both taxes continues.

5008. The other topic that arises here is the interaction between direct tax structures and those taxes within the framework of GATT and similar initiatives. As the Uruguay Round of GATT talks slowly progresses, so the prospect of a new GAS, General Agreement on Services, seems more probable. If the multilateral tariff-reducing approach spreads to services, it will interact clearly not only with VAT rules but also direct tax rules. It will, for example, affect the growing adoption of withholdings on the earnings of sports personalities and entertainers in other states. If the services covered also cover the provision of finance and credit, the interaction is obvious. At present, the interaction between direct tax treaties and GATT remains largely hidden. Its extent was explored, as noted above, in connection with the complaints initiated by the United States against

France, Belgium and the Netherlands about their source-based tax systems. The overlap was confirmed and the concern registered, but as yet no answers to this fundamental challenge to the relative ranking of direct and indirect taxes have been discovered.

5009. One consequence of current trends is that these overlaps will grow. Thought will clearly have to be given to this problem, and any effects that direct tax agreements have on indirect tax approaches, and vice versa. In many states this will cause problems both for administrators and for taxpayers, because of the traditions of treating the two forms of tax separately. The argument must be that that approach is being eroded both practically and conceptually and will, in due course, be highly questionable.

Chapter 6

Patterns of income flows

Everything flows, nothing stays
Heraclitus (quoted in Plato, Cratylus)

600. The practical measure of any effects caused by double taxation agreements or other forms of tax arrangement lies in the changes made to income flows between states party to an agreement, or the inflows or outflows resulting from a unilateral measure. Changes will be of two kinds: the changes on a particular transaction and, as a result of any such changes, a change in the total flows of trade, services, capital and labour between the two states.

Quantifying trade flows

601. As was announced when the United States of America and India recently concluded a double taxation agreement, the assumption is often that a new agreement will stimulate flows between states markedly. Although a number of informal inquiries were made about the availability of such information, none was forthcoming directly on this point, and a number of sources indicated that they were aware of no such figures in the public domain. Neither from them nor from published sources did we hear of any sustained published attempt to measure the effects of double taxation agreements or other similar tax measures, on the flows of goods, services or capital between states.

602. This absence of figures did not unduly surprise. Trade figures are, of course, available in considerable detail between states. Isolating from these figures any meaningful data on the effects of tax measures on flows, except at the very broad level, seems a very difficult task, and certainly one beyond our competence even if, as is unlikely for many key areas, sufficient information is in the public domain. One can, of course, point to end results of policies, such as the over-large financial sector in Luxembourg (as the OECD have done), or the obvious past successes of some tax havens. Even there the recent controversies over drug fund laundering make one wary about how far funds in, for example, a tropical tax haven are the results of treaty-based avoidance tactics rather than 'hot' money.

A model-based approach

603. In the absence of such information, and bearing in mind the problems, an attempt was made to establish an alternative route to meeting the challenge put down by Owens in her paper in 1963 to 'count the dollars',that is, to quantify the effects of a given provision in a double tax arrangement. The method was to construct a number of simple and stylised models of income flows between countries in order to see whether, and if so how, tax reform measures are likely to be changing patterns of flow between states. Like most models, they may seem at one remove – perhaps several – from the real world. They are set on a number of assumptions designed to remove all variables other than those being examined.

604. The approach adopted is to look at the effect on particular kinds of income flow of changes in the marginal rates of tax (0% representing exclusion from the tax base) of the taxes examined. Each example examines the effect on the last 1000 units of value moved through different situations at different levels of tax rate.In doing this, the aim is to examine some of the most obvious trends in recent reforms: the cutting of direct tax rates, and the shifting of tax burdens to general sales taxes or VAT. The text sets out some models and their assumptions, the results arrived at, and a summary of the points raised. How were the models chosen?

A basis for models used

605. We started with the simplest example of traditional international trade. Take two states. A company in each exports goods worth 1000 units of value to the other, at the same time. Assuming equal overheads on the two companies, the companies will make the same profits if, but only if, the tax systems of the two countries are the same (and also assuming no distortion caused by foreign exchange rates and costs). Likewise, the two governments will receive the same net tax receipts.

606. How does this alter if one of the two states alters its tax rates, but the other does not? What is the position if one relies on high direct taxes, and a low sales tax, whilst the other has lowered its direct taxes but imposed a high-level VAT? The model can be made somewhat more realistic by adding in further elements, for example by adding the assumption that the exporting company from state A has a permanent establishment in State B.

607. Time, and the limits on our competence, prevented us from going very far down this road. Nonetheless, it is suggested that it is an approach which may have some value in helping identify the effects of reforms, not

least because it allows what one might term a 'time warp' analysis. By this we mean a comparison of a state's tax systems both before and after reforms. For example, if 1000 units of value were exported from Britain in 1968 to Britain in 1988, with 1000 units also being exported by the reverse route, would the result be neutral, or would one benefit at the cost of the other?

608. It may be objected that these models are oversimplifying the real world. Indeed, they do. In practice business decisions deal with risks, including risks of costs, and have to take account of all sorts of overheads including taxes at several levels of operation, such as social security taxes. Whilst this is, of course, true the point will be more valid, say, for a domestic goods manufacturer than an investment adviser. Even so, this approach does help establish the effects of double tax arrangements even if, in the real world, the distortion effects become submerged below larger, non-tax, considerations.

Model 1: Export of goods from State A to State B

Assume:
A sale of goods from a company resident in State A to a company in State B at arms' length, the companies being independent; profits made by the importing company are ignored. The State A company has no presence in State B, and is not owned by State B nationals. Production costs of goods in State A are 1000. Production bears VAT/GST at its main rate on the full value – rebated on export fully. The company in State A bears corporate income tax at the main rate on its full profits. Profit on the sale is 100. There is no relevant state and local taxation.

This simple example is matched with a simple set of rates:

	Range of rates:				Symbol:
(A)	CT	50	VAT	10	LH
(B)	CT	40	VAT	20	AA
(C)	CT	30	VAT	30	HL

[The symbols are used in the tables below as shorthand for the varying rate structures]

611. This represents in a stylised and highly simplified way, the shift from low rates of indirect taxes combined with high direct rates to low rates being associated with a rise in the rate of VAT. The VAT collected relates to the added value which, set at 100, is equal to the profit.

612. This choice of rate structure has been chosen because it is revenue neutral in State A. This is because the corporate income tax profits at 50% on a profit of 100 produce 50, whilst the VAT on turnover of 1000 produces 100 added value and therefore tax of 10, totalling 60. The other two structures produce the same total revenue, for example the corporate income tax rate of 30% will produce 30, and the VAT at 30% will also produce 30 assuming no international element. (The main limit in practice on this analysis is that items are excepted from charge to tax on the cost of production – chiefly labour costs, and that there are relevant deductions from corporate profits).

613. Given these three different rate structures, nine different sets of relationships between the two states occur if each is free to choose any of the rate structures, as shown:

TABLE 1

Model (and symbols)	STATE A VAT%	CT%	STATE B VAT%	CT%
1 LH -> HL	10	50	30	30
2 AA -> HL	20	40	30	30
3 HL -> HL	30	30	30	30
4 LH -> AA	10	50	20	40
5 AA -> AA	20	40	20	40
6 HL -> AA	30	30	20	40
7 LH -> LH	10	50	10	50
8 AA -> LH	20	40	10	50
9 HL -> LH	30	30	10	50

Results derived from model 1

614. Table 2 shows the application of the model to a transfer of goods on the basis set out that State A – the exporting state - rebates all VAT at export and State B collects VAT on the full value at its main rate. It notes the amount of tax collected or rebated by the state authorities ('fisc') and the amount kept by the company in state A.

TABLE 2

MODEL NO. VAT/CT	FISC.	STATE A CO.	STATE B FISC.
1 LH -> L	– 50	50	330
2 AA -> HL	–160	60	330
3 HL -> HL	–270	70	330
4 LH -> AA	– 50	50	220
5 AA -> AA	–160	60	220
6 HL -> AA	–270	70	220
7 LH -> LH	– 50	50	110
8 AA -> LH	–160	60	110
9 HL ->–LH	–270	70	110

615. What is the significance of the different rate structures?

(a) *To the company in State A:*
Since there is no branch, fixed base or permanent establishment, double taxation does not arise. VAT is fully rebated on exports and no export taxes or custom duties are levied. Therefore the cost in fiscal terms for the company (assuming that the VAT is pushed wholly on to the consumer) is the same whether it produces and sells domestically or it produces domestically and then exports. Company profits, as normal, vary inversely with the rate of corporate income tax. VAT is neutral.

(b) *To State A, the state of residence:*
Because there is no double taxation, double taxation relief measures do not apply. Therefore no corporate income tax is 'lost' when the goods are exported. However because VAT is fully rebate on exports, much revenue is given up when goods are exported. From the results, when the tax collected from domestic transactions is compared to that when goods are exported, the value in revenue terms of VAT can readily be appreciated. The amount of tax collected/lost is dependent on the rate of VAT – no other variables apply.

(c) *To State B, the source state:*
No corporate income tax is collected due to the absence of a permanent establishment. VAT is collected on the goods and therefore revenue collected varies directly with the rate of VAT. This has no effect on the company if it is right to assume that the cost of the VAT is pushed wholly on to the consumer.

Model 2: *Export of goods where exporting company has a permanent establishment in importing state*

616. Assume:

A sale of goods from a company resident in State A to a company in State B at arms' length, the companies being independent; profits made by the importing company ignored. The State A company has a permanent establishment (a branch, not a separate entity) in State B. The company is not owned by State B nationals. Production costs of goods in State A are 1000. Production bears VAT/GST at main rate on full value rebated on export fully. The company in State A bears corporate income tax at the main rate on its full profits in State B (that is, it is assumed that all the profit on the transaction is earned in State B, and none of it is apportioned to State A) and, subject to this tax, in State A. Profit on the sale is 100. State A gives double tax relief to the company in respect of corporate income tax paid in State B. There is no relevant state and local taxation, or branch tax.

Results derived from model

617. Table 3 shows the results of applying this model to the same set of rate structures as Table 1.

TABLE 3

MODEL NO. VAT/CT	STATE A FISC.	STATE A CO.	STATE B FISC.
1 LH -> HL	– 80	50	360
2 AA -> HL	–190	60	360
3 HL -> HL	–300	70	360
4 LH -> AA	– 90	50	260
5 AA -> AA	–200	60	260
6 HL -> AA	–300	60	260
7 LH -> LH	–100	50	160
8 AA -> LH	–200	50	160
9 HL -> LH	–300	50	160

618. These figures suggest:

(a) *To the company in State A:*

VAT is again neutral if we assume that the cost is pushed wholly on to the consumer. It is fully rebated on exports. Therefore the only applicable tax is corporate income tax. Because of the existence of the permanent establishment double taxation occurs, and relief is granted by the state of residence using, we have assumed, the credit method.

(b) *To State A, the state of residence:*
This loses significantly in each case because it both rebates the VAT and credits State B's corporate income tax. In effect, it is left with no claim to tax its resident, but with large rebates on the exported goods.

(c) *To State B, the source state:*
This gains significantly in all cases, collecting both the VAT and the corporate profit tax.

619. A comparison of these two sets of result, together with the tax burden and take if the transfer is purely domestic to State A, starts to reveal the extent to which the different rate structures work to the benefit or detriment of any of those involved. It is clear immediately, however, that the adoption of a destination-based VAT, whilst neutral to internal transfers, is the major factor when exports are being taxed. Were VAT to transfer to an origin-based system as advocated by the European Commission, these figures would look much more similar to the internal figures.

Application to reverse transactions

620. To get a fuller picture of the flows through a treaty, we need to add a further dimension to the model, by allowing flows in both directions. In order to see how the 'balance' of a treaty provision works on sales as different rate structures are adopted, compare the patterns assuming a company in each state exports to the other at the same time, on the basis given.

These may be termed reverse transactions, that is, each transac tion is countered by a reverse identical transaction. The objective is to note through that any unevenness of trade flows caused by the varying rate structures.

621. Table 4 shows the reverse transactions between companies in State A and State B as applied to Model 1 , that is, straight cross-exports of identical amounts.

TABLE 4

MODEL NO. VAT/CT	STATE A FISC.	STATE A CO.	STATE B FISC.	STATE B CO.
1 LH <-> HL	60	50	60	70
2 AA <-> HL	60	60	60	70
3 HL <-> HL	60	70	60	70
4 LH <-> AA	60	50	60	60
5 AA <-> AA	60	60	60	60
6 HL <-> AA	60	70	60	60
7 LH <-> LH	60	50	60	50
8 AA <-> LH	60	60	60	50
9 HL <-> LH	60	70	60	50

(Strictly, of course, the rate structure in 9 is the reverse of 1, that at 2 with 6, and that at 4 with 8, and in reversible actions it matters not which way the data are presented, but for the sake of uniformity the pattern of nine rate structures is maintained).

622. This table suggests that a company subject to one pattern of rate structure can gain as against a company subject to another structure, but that the two tax authorities will be indifferent to this for purely fiscal reasons, as they do not benefit. The revenue collected is always 60 units. This is an arbitrary amount based on the assumptions inbuilt into the model (namely, that the rate structure is 10 and 50, 20 and 40 or 30 and 30). The gainer or loser is the company, which gains or loses because of the corporate income tax rate, VAT being neutral. It will be recalled, in noting this, that the rate structure operates neutrally within one state. The implication is that a state with a higher VAT rate and a lower corporate income tax rate gives an advantage to its companies when trading internationally at no net revenue cost to itself if all other things are equal.

623. What if the exporting company has a permanent establishment in the other state (model 2)? How much tax will be collected by the two states in such a case, as compared with the absence of a permanent establishment? This is shown in Table 5. At the same time, the tax collected by the two states on identical internal transfers may be noted. On the assumptions of the model, this will be 60 in all cases on one transaction.

TABLE 5

MODEL NO. VAT/CT	STATE A PE	NO	STATE B PE	NO
1 LH <-> HL	80	60	60	60
2 AA <-> HL	70	60	60	60
3 HL <-> HL	60	60	60	60
4 LH <-> AA	70	60	60	60
5 AA <-> AA	60	60	60	60
6 HL <-> AA	60	60	70	60
7 LH <-> LH	60	60	60	60
8 AA <-> LH	60	60	70	60
9 HL <-> LH	60	60	80	60

624. The variation in amount of revenue collected between the position where the company has a permanent establishment in the other state, and when it does not, represents the combined sum of the revenue gained from corporate taxation of profits derived from the permanent establishment and the revenue lost in granting double taxation relief when the reverse transaction takes place. Since the credit method is used and the credit is limited to the rate of the resident state's taxation the revenue collected will always be at least equal to that where there is no permanent establishment.

625. More revenue is collected when the resident state's tax rate is higher than that of the source state and this is where the differences arise. Therefore, the highest tax arises in a reverse transaction involving a high corporate income tax state and a low corporate income tax state, and in those cases excess tax is suffered because of the cross-frontier nature of the transactions. This occurs in *all* cases of rate mismatches, and disappears if the two states have the same rate structure, be it high or low. This suggests that there are fiscal advantages to some states if different states have different patterns of tax rate, which will disappear if other states alter their tax rates to the same pattern as those of the 'gainer' state.

626. Table 6 repeats the analysis of Table 5, but showing the post-tax profits made by the companies.

TABLE 6

MODEL NO.	STATE A		STATE B		DOMESTIC	
VAT/CT	PE	NO	PE	NO	A	B
1 LH <-> HL	50	50	50	70	50	70
2 AA <-> HL	60	60	60	70	60	70
3 HL <-> HL	70	70	70	70	70	70
4 LH <-> AA	50	50	50	60	50	60
5 AA <-> AA	60	60	60	60	60	60
6 HL <-> AA	60	70	60	60	70	60
7 LH <-> LH	50	50	50	50	50	50
8 AA <-> LH	50	60	50	50	60	50
9 HL <-> LH	50	70	50	50	70	50

627. This presents the converse picture to Table 5. Due to the existence of a permanent establishment double taxation occurs, relieved by the credit method. This leaves the company paying directly or indirectly the higher of the two rates of tax. As a consequence, companies lose out because they are exporting in some situations. There is in fiscal terms no advantage in operating through a permanent establishment. In the case of the reverse transaction involving a high corporate income tax country, especially when the resident state is a low tax country, the difference is substantial. This suggests that, all other things being equal, the rate structure itself would give relative advantages to some companies in direct interstate competition for markets.

Conclusions from trade models

628. It will be recalled that the model used, with the given rate structures, was revenue neutral as between the different rate structures when operated internally to one state. The tables show that this neutrality is lost when the transactions cross frontiers between countries with differing rate structures, if relief is given by tax credit on the VAT already paid at export on the lines of the standard mechanism for European-style VAT. This provides full relief, whilst the credit-based direct tax relief provides only partial cover where tax rates are not the same in the two states.

629. Distortions therefore occur to the extent that a common rate structure is not adopted by states for corporate income tax – although VAT rates do not affect this equation. Where one state adjusts its systems by shifting from higher corporate income taxes to higher VAT, but the other does not, trading profits of some companies will be affected, and therefore trade will be distorted as noted. It follows that the alteration of the rate structure may itself give a competitive advantage to one state as against another. The conclusion, it is suggested, from the above tables is that a situation where some states trade a reduction of corporate income

tax against increased VAT on a neutral basis internally will be of advantage to the state or its companies (and sometimes both) externally if other states do not introduce the same reform.

630. It must again be stressed that the situation set in the example is highly artificial, and, in particular, the basic underlying trading patterns between two states may be such when they negotiate a treaty that they do not expect balanced flows of trade, and again that other, suppressed, factors in practice totally outweigh the factors identified here.

631. Nonetheless, given the trend to VAT noted above, and given that a significant number of states have made a VAT/corporate income tax trade-off (or have achieved that effect by indirect means),the conclusion may be offered that inter-state competition will put pressure on other states to adopt the reformed pattern. Further, it will for that reason be harder for a state to adopt a reverse reform. This is important because it argues for both a convergence to a new form of rate structure, and for stability of that rate structure once adopted (unless, of course, other assumptions are changed, or states go in for further rounds of cutting corporate income tax as against VAT).

632. In the changes noted in previous chapters, the most important one running against this conclusion is the proposal by the European Commission that VAT become an origin-based tax. It should also be noted that this analysis assumes a credit-based system of double tax relief. Exemption will remove some of the distortions noted because it will not seek to tax foreign source income to the corporate income tax of the state of residence.

Application of trading models to actual situations

633. To test the models, having established their patterns, in actual situations requires the application to them of the current rate and tax structures of actual states. A limited exercise of this nature was attempted with reference to the United Kingdom and selected treaty partners : France (an EC country); the United States of America (a low tax, non-VAT country); Australia (which has just overhauled its system); and India (a developing state with a high reliance on indirect taxes). As a check, we also added United Kingdom (1979), that is, the United Kingdom with the tax rates and regimes it had in 1979, before current reforms were undertaken.

634. The rates operative in those countries are taken as:

COUNTRY	VAT RATE	CT RATE	WT (ON INTEREST)
UK (1989)	15	35	(0)
UK (1979)	8	52	(0)
AUSTRALIA	0	39	10
FRANCE	18.6	37	0
INDIA	0	43.2	15
USA^	0	34	0

Note that the rates are those set at 1 January 1990, and the withholding tax rates are from the relevant double tax agreement with the United Kingdom (1989). (^): The United States of America is shown first (F) charging the federal rate of tax only. In practice many states also charge a local corporate income tax (and the significance of many locally-imposed taxes is growing). On that basis, tax planning by multi-national companies often includes a notional rate for local tax (giving, in one case known to us, a planning rate of 42%, and in another, a planning rate of 40%). Although for some taxpayers such local rates of tax are unavoidable, they are avoidable for others. To make the contrast USA (FS) uses a 40% planning rate, assuming an effective 6% state taxation rate. To adjust the other assumptions, it must also be assumed that double taxation relief is available in the United Kingdom by the credit method for the state taxation paid (as is usually the case by unilateral relief).

635. Table 7 shows results using those rates on Model 1, that is, with a direct export from one state to the other, and reciprocal 'reverse transactions'.

TABLE 7

	TRADING PARTNER				UK (1989)			
	FISC.		CO.		FISC.		CO.	
UK (1979)	60	(140)	48	(48)	50	(190)	65	(65)
AUSTRALIA	39	(39)	61	(61)	50	(190)	65	(65)
FRANCE	56	(242)	63	(63)	50	(190)	65	(65)
INDIA	43	(43)	57	(57)	50	(190)	65	(65)
USA (F)	34	(34)	66	(66)	50	(190)	65	(65)
USA (FS)	40	(40)	60	(60)	50	(190)	65	(65)

Fully domestic transactions are shown in brackets.

Results

636. If all export taxes and customs duties are ignored (as well as the other assumptions inbuilt into the model) the above results are obtained. They show the United Kingdom government's share of transaction is in a 'middle of the road' position, gaining against two partners but losing against the other two. At the company level, the United Kingdom (1989) company does consistently well. However, the model ignores taxes that will prove significant, especially in the case of trade with India and other non – EEC countries. In the case of India, all states impose sales taxes, and the federal government imposes inter-state sales taxes as well as import taxes, so that the Indian fiscal take will increase at the expense (it is assumed here) of the customer. Likewise any goods and services taxation in Australia is ignored, and any state sales taxes, etc, in the United States of America.

637. It is interesting to note that the Fisc under United Kingdom (1989) now collects 10 units less revenue than United Kingdom (1979), though the corporate income tax rate has dropped 17% points, the differencc being made up of the 7% increase in the VAT rate (from 8 to 15%). Also interesting is the difference in the amount of revenue collected by the United Kingdom and France (countries which have VAT) and the United States of America (no VAT). Company profits vary inversely to the corporate income tax rate in the resident state. The amount the United Kingdom (1989) Fisc and company receives is the same, irrespective of the trading partner, since no double taxation occurs and VAT is, it is assumed, fully rebated on exports and charged on imports.

638. Table 8 now applies those same rates and structures to Model 2, that is, to the situation where the exporter has a permanent establishment in the state importing the goods.

TABLE 8

	TRADING PARTNER				UK (1989)			
	FISC.		CO.		FISC.		CO.	
UK (1979)	77	(60)	48	(48)	50	(50)	48	(65)
AUSTRALIA	43	(39)	61	(61)	50	(50)	61	(65)
FRANCE	58	(58)	63	(63)	50	(50)	61	(65)
INDIA	51	(51)	57	(49)	50	(50)	45	(65)
USA (F)	34	(34)	65	(66)	51	(50)	65	(65)
USA (FS)	40	(40)	49	(60)	50	(50)	65	(65)

639. For United Kingdom (1989) revenue receipts there is no variation between the two models, except in trade with the United States of America. This is because it is assumed that VAT is rebated on exports and charged on imports; corporate income tax is collected from the resident company and charged on the profits derived from the permanent establishment of non-resident companies. Since UK (1989)'s corporate income tax rate is lower than all the other countries (except the United States of America, federal rate only, by 1%) double taxation relief is for the full United Kingdom corporation tax paid (in the case of the United States of America, 34/35ths). Generally (United States of America excepted) this results in United Kingdom resident corporations which export paying the other states' rates of tax when operating through a permanent establishment. The effect is that, when rates drop for corporate income tax, but are replaced by a tax such as VAT, which is assumed to be strictly neutral to exporting goods, the company exporting bears tax at the higher rate applicable if it is trading with a state which has not reduced its rates. That is, it does not benefit from the reform as it would internally. The Treasury of the lower-rate state, however, forfeits the tax sacrificed on reducing the rate. It will only gain (as with the United Kingdom against the United States of America) if the other state had reduced its rates even further.

640. Converse pressures apply to companies based in higher rate countries. When double taxation occurs and the credit method is employed, it is immaterial where a company is resident if it has to operate through a permanent establishment and is trading in a lower tax state. The examples suggest that there will be strong pressures to ensure rough equality of corporate rates between states for goods and services trading purposes. Note the large contrast in revenue collected when VAT, and non-VAT countries are compared – United Kingdom (1989) and the United States of America being a comparison which makes this point. Again, especially with India, this is because local sales taxes are ignored, though in practice this will not occur.

The time-warp position

641. The results gained from transactions between United Kingdom (1989) and United Kingdom (1979) are quite revealing. Because of the higher rate of corporation tax in United Kingdom (1979) the revenues gain quite significantly in cross trading. However when compared to revenue collected from domestic transactions the reverse is true. The discrepancy is accounted for by the revenue from the increased VAT rate. Taken overall, it nonetheless remains that, on the basis of our model, the United Kingdom (1989) structure is preferable to the United Kingdom

(1979) structure, and therefore the United Kingdom is a more attractive business base as a result of subsequent developments.

642. The explanation lies partly in the imposition of VAT , which the model assumes is passed on entirely to the customer, whilst the corporate income tax is absorbed entirely by the company, and also in that the model, in looking a the last 1000 units taxed, ignores any changes in the taxable transactions of the company which increase its exposure to corporate income tax, thus raising its average rate, whilst reducing its marginal rate. In practice, the validity of each of those assumptions will vary from one company to another, depending in part on how competitive their particular sector of the market is.

A dividend payment model

643. The other flow we attempt to examine is cross-border flows by way of dividend from one company to another.This is not as straightforward as the previous trade models because of the wide variety of systems in use by states. To try and construct something which could schematically represent what is happening in terms of tax reform in developed states, a series of different positions must be examined.

644. Each of the sub-models takes the case of a dividend value 1000 paid by a company resident in State A to a shareholder in State B. The model was designed to deal with four variable tax rates:

the corporate income tax rate in State A,
the withholding rate in A, if any,
the corporate income tax (or income tax) rate payable by the shareholder in State B and, where relevant,
the income tax rate in State A.

645. The latter is relevant where it is used, as in the United Kingdom, as the basis for awarding imputation credits or, in the United Kingdom, Advance Corporation Tax credits, or foreign tax credits. The sub-models dealt with each of the following methods of applying tax to the corporation and its shareholder, and the double tax relief, if any, arising under the double tax agreement or unilateral system of relief:

1 State A imposes a classical system of taxing profits and dividends;
State B allows a foreign tax credit
up to the level of domestic tax payable in respect of any withholding tax imposed by State A

In this model, both state A's tax rates, and state B's tax rates can be varied.

2 As 1, but State B also allows for underlying relief by credit in respect of the corporate income tax payable on the profits in State A.

3 State A has an imputation system similar to that in the United Kingdom system, and grants full tax credit to an overseas shareholder at an assumed income tax rate (for ACT purposes) of 35% – broadly, a full imputation system;
State B grants a full credit for withholding and underlying tax
Other rates of tax can be varied

4 As model 3, but with State A's income tax set at 25% (in other words, as contrasted with Model 3, this is a partial imputation system).

5 As Model 3, with 35% rate, but with credit being granted by State A for half the tax credit only (a full imputation system with partial credit)

6 As Model 5, but with a 25% income tax rate in State A (a partial imputation system with partial credit)

7 As Model 3, with 35% rate, but with no underlying tax relief from State B (full imputation system with full credit)

8 As 7, with 25% rate (as Model 4, without underlying relief) (partial imputation system with full credit)

9 As Model 7, with 35% rate, but with half tax credit only (as Model 5 without underlying relief)
(partial imputation system with full credit)

10 As Model 9, but with 25% rate (as Model 6 without underlying relief)
(partial imputation system with full credit)

646. In each case the models can also be adjusted to reflect the position where the company in State A, the source state, retained 50% of its profits, only distributing the balance. In each case also, the model can be applied to any combination of any chosen rate for source state corporate income tax, any level of withholding tax by the source state, and any level

of corporate or personal income tax imposed by State B, the state of residence of the recipient of the dividend. The result is a fairly comprehensive range of possibilities for two kinds of system: the classical system, and an imputation system both a full imputation system and a partial system along the lines of the United Kingdom system (but with varying levels of ACT or tax credit provided through the treaty). Even so, this does not accommodate other kinds of split rate or imputation system.

Results from dividend models

647. The results of the models, as applied to two sets of conditions, are set out as Graphs A to E. This is because all the relevant relationships (once the variables are limited to two for any one graph) are linear. The two sets of conditions chosen are intended, as above, to depict the main shift of the tax reform from a higher rate of corporate income tax to a lower rate. For this reason, the main rate of corporate income tax in state A, the source state, is taken at 50% and then at 35%. Graph A shows the position for all ten systems, assuming full distribution of profits, if the source state, has a 50% corporate income tax rate, that is, the pre-reform model, whilst Graph B shows the change when that rate is lowered to 35%. Graphs C and D show the 'before' and 'after' position where half the relevant profits are retained by the company. Graph E emphasises the contrasts shown by displaying a selection of 'before' and 'after' results against each other.

648. The horizontal axis of each graph indicates the rate of corporate or personal income tax set by the state of residence of the recipient of the dividend (state B). The level of withholding applied by the source state (state A, from which the company paying the dividend pays it) is accommodated by shifting the zero point of the horizontal axis by one unit for each percentage point of the withholding. This is because the effect of different levels of withholding tax is to shift the starting point at which the state of residence starts collecting tax, but does not thereafter affect the marginal yield, because in all cases the state of residence of the recipient of the dividend is assumed to give full credit for the withholding tax. The main axis of the graph assumes a 15% withholding tax. Accordingly, the position where there is no withholding tax is represented by shifting the horizontal axis of the graph 15 units to the right (as indicated).

649. The vertical axis of each graph indicates the number of units of tax collected by state B, the state of residence of the recipient of the dividend, for every 1000 units of profit earned and (on the assumption of graphs A and B) distributed.

Graph A: source state with 50% tax

650. The graph depicts the tax collected by the state of residence of the recipient of the dividend at any given level of corporate (or personal) income tax in that state as adjusted to reflect each of the ten combinations of choice of corporate tax system and treaty credit provision. The graph shows that the system most productive of tax for the residence state, at any given level of corporate or personal income tax, is Model 7, the case where the source state has a full imputation system and grants the credit to foreigners, but the residence state of the dividend recipient restricts its grant of credit to the tax directly imposed by the source state on the dividend, not on the underlying profits. By contrast, the least favourable position for the state of residence of the dividend recipient is Model 2, where the source state has a classical system of corporate taxation, and the residence state grants credit for both the tax on the dividend and the underlying tax. All other forms of system lie at some intermediate point to these systems for all levels of residence state tax and source state withholding.

651. It will be noted that, although the relationships between the variables are linear for any one system of tax and credit, the lines do not all lie at the same angle on the graph, that is, the relationships are not identical even excluding different starting points. It will also be noted just how wide is the spread between the lines. Under Model 7, the state of residence starts collecting tax once its corporate income tax rate exceeds 9% (assuming a 15% withholding by the source state). But under model 2, no tax will be collected by the residence state on all these assumptions unless it puts its corporate income tax rate at the least at 58% – a rate higher than even the pre-reform rates in most states. The inference is that a system similar to Model 2 will in effect, if not in name, be an exemption system, where the source state rates are at about 50% or more. However, were the state to withdraw the underlying relief, the effect would change sharply – to that of Model 1 – and tax would be collected once the rate crossed 16%.

652. Finally, if the residence state has dropped its rates to below 49%, it will only collect tax at more than 5% if its models do not include Models 3 and 4 as well as 2.

Graph B: source state with 35% tax

653. Graph B has the same axes as Graph A, and examines the same models but for the assumption that the rate of corporate income tax in the source state, from which the dividend is paid, is reduced to 35% (not 50% as in A). This therefore allow us to compare the position where the source state has reduced its main corporate income tax rate.

645. As might be anticipated, the chief difference between Graph B and Graph A is the angle of slope of the lines, which has increased to compensate for the lower levels of tax being collected in the source state. However, this is not the only effect, because the starting point of some of the lines has also shifted. Model 7 is again the most advantageous system for the state of residence, as might be expected, whilst both models 2 and 3 (that is the model of source state with classical system and residence state with underlying tax relief, and also the model of a full imputation system with underlying relief) are shown as disadvantageous.

655. If the residence state reduces its corporate tax rate to 35% along with the source state, it will receive no tax using either models 2 or 3, or 4 (which is the same as 3 except that there is only a partial imputation).

656. By way of comparison of the two graphs, at the extreme of Model 7 (imputation with no underlying relief by the state of residence), the yield to the state of residence levying a rate of 50% rises from 310 per 1000 units of dividend where the source state has a tax rate of 50% and a withholding of 15% to 410. If it wished to maintain its yield, the state of residence could alternatively afford to cut its rate of tax to 40%. If it reduced its rate to 35% in line with the source state it would sacrifice 50 (or 5%). This position would be changed sharply by any change in the withholding tax. If that were reduced from 15% to 5% without any other offsetting changes, the state of residence would receive a yield of 410 on a 35% rate. It would even receive a yield of 50 (or 5%) on the most disadvantageous tax system.

657. The graphs also show, for example, that if the source state cuts its tax rate from 50% to 35% and the withholdings are reduced to 10% from 15% and which has a full imputation system, the state of residence could also afford to cut its tax rate on that transaction from 50% to 26% if it granted no underlying relief, – more than any likely cut. This reflects the sensitivity of the balance between source states and residence state to any withholding tax.

Graph C: source state with 50% tax rate, and only half profits distributed

658. Graph C again has the same axes and assumptions as Graph A, except that in this case the corporate income tax rate in the source state is retained at 50%, but the company in the source state retaining half the profits there, and distributes only half of its available profits. The vertical axes indicates the level of profits, not therefore the level of distributions. The assumption of the graph is again a complete one, whilst it might be anticipated in practice that the level of withholding would reflect,

amongst other matters, the relative as well as absolute levels of tax. It may also be noted that this graph is limited, as compared with Graph A, because none of the models reflects a split-rate corporate tax system.

659. As compared with Graph A (full distribution) Graph C shows, as one would expect, a sharp drop in the levels of tax collected by the state of residence for any given amount of profit in the source state. But it also shows that the rate of drop is not the same for all systems of tax. That is, Graph C is not just a reproduction of graph A with different slopes angles to the lines, indicating that the amount of tax collected is not merely half that which would have been collected on a full distribution. Rather, it shows a more complicated interrelationship. What is more, it shows that the most productive model of a tax system for the state of residence is not the same as that where there is full distribution, unless the state of residence has a tax rate exceeding 60% – which is most unlikely. It also shows that any of the models 2, 3, 4, 5 or 6 will yield very little tax to the state of residence unless it has a tax rate of over at least 45% so long as the source state maintains a 50% rate, at least if the withholding rate remains at 15%.

Graph D: source state with 35% rate, and half profits withheld

660. Graph D also has the same axes and scale but, like Graph C it shows the case of 50% profit retention, with the source state corporate income tax at 35%, rather than 50%. This shows a pattern broadly similar to Graph C, with no one relationship between the tax level on full distribution and that on half distribution, except that the yield to the state of residence at any given corporation tax rate is higher.

661. As just noted, the residence state will yield no tax at all with a tax rate of 40% or lower either from model 2 (source state with classical system and residence state granting underlying relief) or from models 3, 4,5 or 6 (these are all forms of imputation system, full or partial, with full or half credit under the double tax agreement, and with underlying relief granted by the state of residence of the recipient of the dividend). In other words, on the assumptions behind both Graph C and Graph D, the grant of underlying relief by the state of residence is the equivalent in practical terms to adopting an exemption system if the residence state tax rate is under 40%, even if the rate of tax in the source state drops to 35%, if there is a 15% withholding. If the withholding was removed in entirety, tax would be yielded to the state of residence under some of these systems once the residence state tax rate exceeded 26%, but even then it would have to exceed 36% if the source state has a classical system and the residence state grants underlying relief.

Some conclusions on dividend flows

662. The models show the effect of a drop in the corporate or personal income tax rate by either or both of the source state where the company paying the dividend is based, or the state of residence of the recipient of the dividend with a company pursuing either a full or a partial distribution policy. In addition to the points noted above, the graphs show clearly the difficulty of assuming that, because the main rates of tax in different states are the same, so also are the taxes collected from dividend flows.

663. Taking graph A as the 'pre-reform' position, it can be seen just how wide a variation of effective levels of tax can occur in the state of residence of the shareholder given a set level of corporate income tax and withholding tax in the source state, and a set level of corporate income tax in the residence state, if variations occur in the presence or absence of imputation, the grant of a full or half credit by the residence state, and the granting or withholding of relief for the underlying tax on the dividend.

664. For example, on graph A, with both states having a corporate income tax of 50%, and a withholding tax at 15%, the 'take' of the residence state can vary from nil to 31% of the dividend. It should be noted that the 'take' of the source state also varies, though this is not represented on the graph, as it is a fixed amount for each model. The width of this variation is also marked, and is as follows (results for assumptions and models in Graph A only):

Model 1	575
Model 2	575
Model 3	306
Model 4	408
Model 5	440
Model 6	492
Model 7	306
Model 8	408
Model 9	273
Model 10	339

This is not shown on each graph, as it would be represented by a horizontal line at the appropriate level on the vertical axis. The only value of showing that line would be to note the combination of rates at which the dividend was totally exhausted by tax, leaving nothing for the dividend's supposed recipient. In practice even on Graph A with a source state rate of 50%, and giving the state of residence the most advantageous (from its standpoint) tax system the exhaustion point will not arise unless the rate of tax of the state of residence is at least 65% and there is a 15% withholding by the source state.

665. The figures for source state 'take' show the same range of 'takes' though with a higher base point, from 27% to 58%. The shareholder will receive the balance after the source state tax take at the above amount, and the variable amount received by the state of residence depending on its corporate income tax rate.

666. Graph A shows the relationship between rates as in all cases linear, with only two variables : the point at which the residence state starts becoming entitled to receive tax, and the marginal rate of collection from that point (represented by the slope of the lines). It will be noted that there is no overall consistency to either of these variables, although the marginal rates do not very markedly on this graph. As one would expect, the tax collected by states allowing underlying tax relief (models 2 to 6) is in all cases noticeably lower than those not allowing that relief (models 1 and 7 to 10).

667. Graph B, showing the same assumptions operating in the 'post-reform' state, that is, with the corporate income tax of the source state dropping to 35%, shows a spread in range, if both states have corporate income taxes at 35%, of nil to 29%, and if the residence state retained a 50% rate whilst the source state has a 35% rate, the range is from 5% to 41%. This suggests that the differences between the methods of allowing offsetting (if any) to handle economic double taxation, and the methods of giving double tax relief under a double taxation agreement, are accentuated post-reform, as are the incremental differences in the different options as the residence state tax rates are increased.

668. Again the 'take' of the source state varies from one model to another, over a range from 10% to 45%, although this is not, as already noted, shown on the graph.

669. The effect in both cases of changing the withholding tax is, as noted above, merely to shift the point at which the residence state starts collecting tax by a set amount directly related to the withholding and not affected by the model of tax system used. Nor does the withholding tax affect the marginal rate of tax in the state of residence.

670. Graphs C and D are provided as a simple 'control' against possible distortions arising from the assumptions of full profits distribution. Clearly a no-distribution policy gives rise to no problems for present purposes (though there may be legislation deeming distribution along CFC

lines in an actual case). These graphs indicate, as one might expect, that the marginal rate of tax collected from a given amount of profits declines sharply.

671. What is less predictable, but becomes clear in graphs C and D is that the forms of source state taxation which yielded the largest take to the residence state on a full-distribution basis do not yield the same full benefit under a half-distribution policy. Further, the lines on the graphs cross in a number of places. This indicates that, on a half-distribution basis, the advantages to the residence state of particular forms of taxation or relief by the source state have become sensitive to the underlying tax rate of the *residence* state.

672. For example, on Graph C (the source state has a 50% corporate income tax), the state of residence gets the highest tax share if the source state has an imputation system with a half-credit, and the residence state concedes no underlying relief (model 9). But if the residence state corporate income tax were to exceed 55%, it would be better with a full credit system (model 7). Most marked is the relative decline in the advantage to the residence state of a source state with a classical system (model 1). At a tax rate of 20% this is relatively attractive to a residence state. But it is noticeably less attractive if its rate is 45% or over.

673. If the scale of the vertical axis of each graph were doubled, so equating the amount *distributed* rather than the amount earned, the marginal rates would become similar, as is shown by graph E. On both graphs C and D the difference between those systems granting underlying relief, and those not, is particularly marked. This suggests there is no qualitative difference between the effective treatment of a partial distribution of profits as against a total distribution.

674. The overall conclusions suggested by these results are that the superficial equality and convergence of tax rates hides a wide divergence of effective tax rates in the context of international double taxation leaving out of account relative withholding rates, profit distribution policies, and also differing definitions of profits and permissible deductions, by reason only of the differing attitudes to imputation and underlying tax, and to the award or refusal of full tax credits.

Who wins and who loses?

675. Whether a state will be a 'gainer' or a 'loser' internationally out of a change in, or a refusal to change, its nominal rates of taxation on corporate profits and dividends will therefore depend to a significant extent on

the particular way in which it accords double taxation relief in such cases. This suggests that the shifts of the main rates of corporate income tax will not be neutral as between states even where the two states make identical changes in rates. This is emphasised by Graph E which compares the 'before' and 'after' rates (ie where the source state rate is 50% and 35%). The particularly sharp advantage to the state of residence which grants underlying relief if the source state drops its rate from 50% to 35% (models 5 (50%) and 6 (35%)) is only enjoyed if the residence state itself has a corporate income tax rate of over 45%, that is, it has not reformed its tax rate.

676. Further interesting conclusions arise if the graphs are reversed against each other, that is, we adopt the same 'reverse transactions' approach as with the trade models. The resultant graphs are not copied here, but they show a wide 'diamond' of possible intersections between graph lines. By this we mean that the point at which State A starts to receive more than State B (that is the lines representing the take of the residence states cross) can vary widely. This emphasises the points made above about the actual effects in particular patterns of tax and relief of changes in nominal rates.

677. In looking for a converging system and one that is likely to have lower corporate and income tax rates, and is more likely to have an imputation system, perhaps we ought also to note the median result of these models, that is the one producing nearest to the average of all the models. This is evidenced on graphs B and D. On graph B (showing full distributions), assuming the residence state has a tax rate of about 35%, that will lie between models 1 and 6, that is, between the source state with a classical system ,with the residence state giving a full credit, and the imputation system where only a half credit is given but the residence state gives underlying relief. On Graph D, showing 50% distribution, the result is less obvious, but lies between model 6 just noted, and model 8 which is a partial imputation system with a full credit and no underlying relief (a pattern adopted by some United Kingdom treaties).

A balance between treaty parties?

678. The question of relative advantages from treaties gives rise to another unknown in relation to public figures: the extent to which current at individual transactions. However, isolated examples do not show if a double taxation agreement is 'balanced' in its provisions, that is, whether it treats the two parties in an even-handed way.

679. To measure that, another approach is suggested following some of the methods applied above, namely that of an assumed flow of trade between the two states. The assumption is that the same flow of funds occurs from each state to the other at the same time. Each of the possible forms of flow of funds under a treaty can be examined to see what happens if funds flow under the rules provided in a reciprocally equal way through all possible routes allowed under the treaty. In each case two sets of taxpayers and two national fiscs are involved. Does any one gain at the expense of others – do the two recipients in one state gain at the expense of the other, or is the deal truly symmetrical?

680. For example, if the two states are A and B, and payment is made by a company of a dividend direct to the shareholder, the routes are AA (from corporation in A to shareholder in A), AB, BA, BB. Each example to be applied with the tax rates and systems of the two states. This is used to calculate separately the tax position for each possible route that the dividends could take. The same could be done for each kind of flow, so that, for example, it could also replicate the models of traded goods used earlier in this chapter.

681. A usual view of 'balance' on transactions is to look at the relative amounts of tax collected by the two states from these transactions. The reverse method is to look at the amount of tax foregone by each state as against the tax that would be collected had the transaction been entirely internal. These, in one sense, reflect the separate points of view of the taxpayer and taxing authority. The one view starts on the assumption that there should be a 'level playing field' as between taxpayers in the two states, whatever the national policies of the two states. The other has traditionally started with the assumption that the given is the national rate of corporate income tax, and that adjustments should be aimed at smoothing the differences between the national rates. It must be said that whilst both are valid viewpoints, the former is more in keeping with the trends of recent tax reforms than the latter. If the reason State A adopts a particular approach to an agreement is that it chooses a high corporate income tax rate with low VAT, whilst the treaty partner adopts the reverse strategy, it must be questioned whether the former state should be assumed, in a modern context, to continue with a higher rate of direct tax protected through a treaty without more.

682. It is suggested that an alternative measure of balance which gives a fuller indication is to see how the two economies fare, that is, to see the total of tax and dividends received both by the investor and by the Treasury in one state rather than the other. The amounts received, as sug-

gested, by the two economies can be measured by comparing the sum of the tax 'take' for each of the two countries together with the net receipts of the taxpayers of the two countries from whichever form of flow is being reviewed. Expressed as a simple formula, the balance is:

$$(T_{uk} + D_{uk}) - (T_{tp} + D_{tp})$$

where T is the tax take of the Treasury, and
D is the net income received in UK or TP (treaty partner)

683. To apply the formula, the net receipt to each of the four recipients (or classes of recipient) is calculated assuming an equal flow of value through each possible route. The balance of the totals is then noted under the above formula. A state may gain, under this analysis, either through the treasury or the taxpayer. This is an important proviso, because there can be a balance of economies even though one taxpayer is paying noticeably higher rates than the other within this balance. What therefore is balanced between economies at the macro level may clearly lead to distortion of trade (and the reverse). That highlights the point made on a number of occasions in this discussion, that a view on double taxation developments must look at the inter-state comparisons as well as the state-taxpayer position. If, as a result of the application of this formula, one state consistently gains at the expense of the other – either in the public sector or the private sector or both – one would look for a balancing feature the other way elsewhere in the agreement or in the context in which the agreement is made. If that balancing factor could not be found, the agreement itself could be said to be imbalancing the trade flows between the states, and therefore not in the best interests of both treaty parties.

684. Echoing what was discussed in the last chapter, it may be noted that the treaty may contain a deliberate imbalance. It may be that the objectives behind a treaty are essentially non-tax, or that one state is prepared to concede an imbalance (particularly a hidden one in terms of the face of the agreement) as part of a larger arrangement between the two states. The authorities in State B, for example, might be prepared to tolerate a net gain by the companies in State A as part of some other deal. Again, one state may be happy to leave one article in a treaty imbalanced against itself or its taxpayers secure in the knowledge that this is of little importance, or because of another imbalance in its favour elsewhere which is more important.

685. In practice, under this full definition of balance, few treaties will be balanced even after the recent reforms. Whilst these have caused reduc-

tion and convergence of rates of underlying taxes, they have effected withholdings little as yet. Further, with particular reference to taxation of dividend flows, there has been only limited convergence in approach to taxation of the distribution of corporate profits. In fact, the balance formula emphasises the reverse. To obtain an inter-state balance where there are wide variations in the methods of tax employed, there must be an appropriate discrepancy in the rates used.

686. This can be illustrated by comparing a classical system with a system of partial imputation such as that used in the United Kingdom, as the following example shows:

Assume the rate of personal income tax in both State A and State B operates at 50%, and that the corporate income tax in State B is 35% (as in the United Kingdom). What is the equivalent rate of corporate income tax in State A so as to secure the same return of taxes on distributed profits in the two states?

State B
Let profit of company C be 100
CT payable in B is therefore 35
Dividend available for distribution is 65
The tax credit, if on the same basis as the United Kingdom, is therefore 22
The investor I will receive (65 + 22)
I pays tax at 50%, so owes (43 – 22) to B
B receives 56 and I receives 44

State A
A must therefore receive 56, to equal B
Let profit of company D be 100
Let corporate income tax rate in A be z%
CT payable in A is therefore z
Dividend available for distribution is (100-z)
The investor J receives this
J pays tax at 50%, so owes (100-z)/2
A therefore receives z + (100-z)/2, whilst J receives (100-z)/2
Therefore: z + (100-z)/2 = 56
This yields: z = 12%

687. In summary, given a consistent personal income tax rate of 50%, and one state with an ACT system and a corporate income tax rate of 35%, another state with a classical system of taxation will require only a rate of 12% to achieve the same fiscal effect. A parallel calculation showing the personal income tax rate to be 25% would yield the result that the corporate income tax rate in state A should be 13%, broadly consistent

with the previous answer, as does the equivalent calculation with a top tax rate of 40%.

General conclusions

688. This chapter has attempted to offer some models and formulae with which to assess in some sort of quantitative way the effects of, and fairness between states of, double tax agreements. Some attempt has been made to show these models at work with real systems, but a fully developed analysis along those lines is beyond the scope of this enquiry. What the chapter may suggest, however, is a way of viewing the effect of double tax treaties as judged against the changing patterns of rates.

689. The findings emphasise the importance of any shift from direct to indirect taxes (or the reverse), the importance of withholding taxes in the re-allocation of income from residence state to source state, and the fact that similar rate structures which gave a superficial view of convergence may in reality be producing a greater divergence and higher levels of imbalances between states if viewed from their operation within typical double tax arrangements.

690. The debate as a whole highlights, it is suggested, two particularly important features : the similarity or disparity of tax structures between two similarly placed states may call for more sophisticated bilateral adjustments than just ensuring the 'right' withholding and, reinforcing that view, that the real effect of withholdings has increased and has created a bigger distortion to the assumed frameworks of double tax treaties than was the case prior to recent reforms, even if it does not increase the overall levels of tax levied. This point is increasingly accepted in recent double taxation agreements, particularly with their elaborate provisions in place of the OECD Model article 10. Further, differences in the system of corporate income taxes used is also accentuated, as are the differences in terms in double taxation agreements dealing with dividends.

691. Finally, this must all be seen against the arguments derived from the examples of flows of goods and services subject to both corporate income tax and VAT. This suggested marked advantages to states adopting lower corporate income tax rates and it was argued that this suggested that the new system would be a stable one, because of the difficulties of reversing it unilaterally. This argues therefore that the reforms charted throughout this chapter are likely to remain.

Chapter 7

The future shape of international taxation

> On résiste à l'invasion des armées; on ne résiste pas à l'invasion des idées
>
> Hugo, Histoire d'un Crime

700. Having reviewed the patterns of taxation that have changed and are emerging, it is appropriate to reflect what alternative patterns of future taxation may develop from them, and to identify areas of difficulty. In writing this part of the essay above all, there is a danger of pretending to see into the future, and one must instantly admit the limits of any such operation. But, as the forester inspecting the new-planted forest can see in his mind's eye the rows of trees that will, unless something untoward occurs, grace the contours he surveys, so – if less certainly – one can note what has happened and argue forward from that. One proviso is, of course, that forest fires, earthquakes, landslips, flooding and the ravages of war are much more likely to affect particular taxes than particular forests.

701. The 'trees' we have seen planted will grow in very fertile ground. It seems that little can stop the steady integration of the developed world's economies. In the last two or three years, most of the economies which have tried to stand apart – like those of Russia and Eastern Europe, Brasil and other South American states, and some of the states of Asia, have found themselves unable to do so. China, perhaps, suffered some reversal since the events of 1989, but even that may be viewed merely as a slowing down for a time. Elsewhere it is only closed societies – usually in democratic terms as well as economic – that have stood aside. Perhaps, for example, Burma might be counted as one of these. Albania, it seems, has ceased so to be in 1990. Some are teetering on bankruptcy. Certainly, and sadly, the economies of several smaller African states are steadily decreasing in real terms. The world economy, it seems, has less to offer them than once it did.

The position in Europe

702. In Europe there is little now to stop the sweep of economic forces that will produce an integrated European economy in due course. There may be disagreement on the speed at which events should occur, but a significant level of integration will occur as a result of events which have already taken place and agreements which have already been put in train. This follows from the decisions under and since the Single European Act, and the momentous changes in central and eastern Europe.

703. The most dramatic of the events in Europe had not been foreseen by anyone at the time the research behind this work was started – a sanguine reminder of the dangers of looking too far ahead. The train of events resulting in and following the merger of the two Germanies, the democratisation of several of the former CMEA states of central and eastern Europe and the effects of perestroika in the USSR, with the ripple effects to other Socialist states elsewhere, has meant, in effect, that one of the variables in world taxation is disappearing. The CMEA is being phased out, and with it presumably the CMEA double tax agreements will in due course fall. They will undoubtedly be replaced with treaties on the OECD lines. Certainly, Hungary and the other central European states were busily engaged in negotiating a network of treaties as soon as they became free to do so.

704. As is evident to observers as much in Cambodia as in Hungary, the 'Soviet model' tax system, with high specific indirect taxes used as price regulators, little use of income and employee social security taxes, and above all little by way of corporate profits taxes, is collapsing. It would seem that in the absence of commands, the tax system of a command economy itself just fades away. Unless the state is to collapse as well, it must be replaced. The model chosen in some of the states is a tax regime deliberately in the form of the Western post-reform model with wide bases, lower rates and a general sales tax along the lines of VAT, plus increased reliance on social security funding taxes.

705. The reforms in Hungary started a few years ago, and were guided by the International Monetary Fund and World Bank economic and administrative experts. They had even greater effect in Poland, which launched a rapid – it proved over-rapid – reform in 1989. The CSFR is also engaged in the same process. The patterns of reform in these countries are particularly important in noting trends. Rarely do countries have to change a complete tax system rapidly. In these states it proved necessary, because the previous system suffered from two unavoidable and fatal

weaknesses. They were the taxes of a command economy not a market economy, and the commands no longer existed.

706. The replacement came on the basis of two main factors ; advice offered by outside experts, as noted, and a desire to see their systems compatible with (it was hoped from the start) eventual membership of the European Communities. EC-style VAT was therefore a must, to replace other price-regulating and enormously complex taxes. A new corporation tax (or in the case of Hungary, an Entrepreneur's Profits Tax applying to all forms of business) was next, with a comprehensive, broad-based, simple and relatively low rate personal income taxes to follow. Social security taxes already existed, but the states are shifting social security obligations more clearly on to a funded basis. Then protection and the protective tariffs will be stripped steadily away. Local taxes will follow, perhaps on a property basis. One other factor can be guaranteed. The costs of modernising the economies of the eastern part of Germany, Poland, Hungary, and the CFSR, let alone the other state of Eastern Europe and the USSR itself, will ensure major tax demands on those states and all those who help for the rest of this decade.

707. What these developments in Europe mean is that over an area encompassing over two dozen countries, including four of the Group of Seven economies, tariff, exchange and other barriers are being taken down, with resultant flows of money and, in descending order, goods, services and people. This is happening with an acute awareness of the pressures this imposes on the individual tax systems and tax administrations of these states. The pattern of indirect tax is already looking increasingly similar throughout the whole continent.

708. At the same time, only hesitant steps have so far been taken to solve problems caused by national direct taxes to trans-national developments such as mergers within the area, or indeed in connection with national direct taxes generally, where the European Commission has limited competence, and states seem reluctant, even in the shadow of the Single Market, to change their ways.

The position in North America

709. The second focus of interest is North America, where both the USA and Canada have had major tax reform efforts, and where their common links have been strengthened by the free trade agreement between them. But to neither of these countries can tax reform mean tax reduction, even in the short term, and there are significant pressures in both for tax increases in some form. Equally, even in these economies the pressures of

the logic of tax reform, which the USA did much to start, are now starting to dictate some of the answers.

710. The Canadian government has adopted corporate tax reforms, and a modified form of a VAT. The US government has not moved yet on either, but is looking at both. The sheer size of its problems over thrifts means that the grand statements in 1988 and 1989 about 'no new taxes' were already embarrassing in 1990. A close look is being taken at the imputation system of corporate taxes again and – yet again – at VAT. It will be painful for the USA of all states to concede to outside pressures, even if it was the USA as much as anyone that started those pressures. But viewed in 1990 it is difficult to see where else the US Federal authorities can turn if they have to raise up to $150 billion unforeseen additional revenue, even before the short-term costs of warfare were added to this.

711. Pending such changes, and constrained to operate existing tax patterns, it is not surprising that the most important trend from the US since the reform package is its aggressive approach to outreach provisions. The USA has a long tradition of 'long-arm' statutes for dealing with foreign companies or individuals who offend what are seen as American interests, and this concern is now being turned to tax. This has led to the branch profits tax and treaty override legislation, aggressive provisions on transfer pricing, and in particular the measures on superroyalties and the like, equally aggressive anti-tax-haven measures, measures to secure greater compliance with its nationality-based world wide tax claims, and general strong assertion of its interests both unilaterally and in the terms of its double tax and double social security treaties, its position in the GATT Uruguay Round and other international measures.

The position in Asia

712. The third important focus is East Asia and Oceana. This has also seen its share of tax reform, and increased aggressiveness by tax authorities. One particular state that has engaged in this is Australia, which has recently taken steps to control tax losses beyond its jurisdiction with legislation on controlled foreign companies and thin capitalisation and an active review of its double tax treaties to cope with what some say is the most aggressive use by taxpayers of fiscal boundaries to avoid tax. Certainly the contrast of style with the taxpayers of Japan and similar states is very marked.

713. In East Asia, although a large uncertainty shrouds speculation about Hong Kong, the economic future of several others looks set to join the developed, rather than developing, cycle. Thus, Japan has hesitantly fol-

lowed the reform pattern of other OECD states, and South Korea is emerging to join both the OECD and the change in tax patterns. Reforms announced by it in 1989 started to take effect in 1990 with an expansion of the scope of the capital gains tax and a reduction of tax rates on smaller businesses. These followed on reforms of the previous year which had included simplification of the income tax rate scales.
The reform also included another variant, the minimum alternative tax as pioneered in the USA.

714. There has also been a steady build-up of double tax treaty links throughout the region. Indonesia has been particularly active in renewing and extending its treaty network (involving in the last two years revised or new treaties with Austria, Finland, Germany, Hungary, Korea, Malaysia, Netherlands,New Zealand, Norway, Sweden, Switzerland and the USA, with others being discussed), and even Hong Kong has concluded its first, limited, agreement. The new Inter-ASEAN model double taxation convention is both an influence on, and a result of, the growth of treaties in this area. It is another derivative of the OECD pattern of model.

715. In West Asia political maturity and growing experience, plus a widened circle of outside advisers, is allowing systems to be developed which are less dependent on colonial heritage – but conversely are more dependent on the demands of developed state trading partners' current approaches. Thus India, in its 1990 budget has adopted a significantly lower corporate income tax rate (down to 43.2% from 54%) offset by a base widening exercise. It has also removed the cascade effect of some of its direct taxes.

The position elsewhere

716. The economies of South America have also been subject to the same trends in reform and integration into the world economy, and several states here have been actively expanding their treaty networks.

717. Perhaps potentially of most significance internally, but of little moment on the world scene, are tax developments in the poorest states of the world. Now that the grandiose post-freedom schemes and dreams have passed on, and bitter economic realities are taking their tolls, some states are more actively considering their tax policies as development tools. Even their combined effects are of no real concern in this study because of the absence of any external effects but the problems still need addressing.

718. This brief suvey, reflecting reforms noted in Chapter 2, confirms that there are few who are not involved in the growing web of tax agreements, and the growing pressures of the world market place on tax systems, whilst at the same time being subject to the growing demands of public finance for higher tax ratios.

Tax havens

719. This survey has paid less attention to one group of states: – the smallest states, the list of which looks much like the list of tax havens. Although Luxembourg and Switzerland are not small in any significant sense, many of the states are, in terms of geography and population. By contrast, their economies are often much larger than the atlas might suggest, due to the growth of offshore tax planning. 'War' was first declared on tax havens in 1961 by President Kennedy. This led only to the Subpart F legislation from the US Congress, although the original aim had been to eliminate havens altogether. How are they faring thirty years later?

720. Two particular trends among the major economies have been noted earlier in this report. First is the toughening up of treaty terms, and the treaty network, to deal with treaty shopping and also to deal with fiscal privileges, together with the termination by some states of some treaties with tax havens. This was intended to dampen the extent to which havens could be used in combination with flows of money through treaty routes. Second is the quickening pace of outreach legislation in developed states to tackle flows of money to and from havens. These have included in particular the adoption of legislation of a Subpart F pattern by most of the major world economies plus the moves on transfer pricing, bank secrecy, conduit companies and other areas studied in detail by the OECD as well as individual states in the last decade. Both are partial answers to the problems presented to major economies by havens.

721. Separately, there has been a greater deployment of tax officials, backed by information exchange provisions and joint audits. But that can only go so far, if initiatives such as the OECD/CE multilateral agreement finds no acceptance.

722. Despite that, the more stable tax havens clearly flourish, as reports that Jersey is 'full up' suggest. Other state are also moving into the field – Malta and Cyprus in the fringes of the European Community; Singapore in Asia. What is more, the technique is increasingly being adopted by the major states within themselves, and in their neighbouring states. Witness the growth of the use of enterprise zones in recent years in Germany,

France, Britain and Belgium, or the privileged areas and companies of Ireland, and reports that the latest recruit, the USSR, is proposing to set up onshore 'offshore' areas to encourage inward investment.

723. The process of imitation has, within the European Community, as we may also note, led to the winding down of, in particular, taxes on capital income – or savings. Once it became clear that Luxembourg was not going to alter its fiscally favourable treatment of interest and investment institutions such as unit trusts, it took little time for the UK, France, Belgium, the Netherlands, Ireland and Germany (and the list may not be complete) to react by cutting some of their own taxes. As with enterprise zones, it was deemed better to keep the money at home by fair competition.

724. This limited tolerance of fiscally privileged areas does not apply to 'hot' money, such as that resulting from the drugs trade. Here, pressures appear to be building up which will suggest much stronger measures. In a sense, tax havens are a side effect of the absolute nature of sovereignty of states in the modern world. If one state, such as the USA, France or the UK, is not prepared to help enforce others' tax systems or to reach multilateral agreements on taxes, then they must watch other states who choose to gain tax revenues by using very low rates. But states have never stood back to this extent when enforcing each others' criminal laws (political and tax offences apart).

725. There is a long tradition of cooperation on many aspects of enforcement of criminal law involving, for example, extradition, mutual collection of evidence and intelligence, and even allowing a prisoner convicted of an offence in a foreign state to serve his sentence in his home state. The perceived threat of the drugs trade means that these forces are being turned against movements of money of dubious origin. This is aimed in part at the international banks that, to quite an extent, make tax havens possible. If they are asked to 'cooperate' in policing flows of illegal money, as is currently being mooted in several places, then one major aspect of havens – their secrecy rules – will be weakened. It is suggested that this is an area where significant action will be seen in future as other states are forced to tackle a problem of the same level of seriousness as that confronting Malaysia today.

726. Weakening is also occurring in other ways, chiefly through the patterns of reform we have been examining in this work. A decrease in tax rates on smaller companies, and the sharp reductions in the top rates of personal income tax make tax havens relatively less attractive. To the extent that these direct taxes are replaced by social security taxes or by

value added tax or other products taxes, the forms of taxation used are themselves less avoidable, or have built in economic considerations to counteract avoidance. VAT is avoided by not consuming; social security taxes avoided at the risk of later losing benefits. No such trade-off exists behind individual or corporate income taxes. If the reforms therefore have marginal advantages in dealing with the non-criminal aspects of tax havens, that will be another element in their success and likely staying power. Perhaps also there may be an element of 'fashion' about tax havens as so much else, and perhaps the psychology of tax reform has, a little, contributed to making havens a little less fashionable.

727. The original select few tax havens have therefore been subjected to a series of pressures : exclusion from the tax treaty networks that gave some of them particular advantages; tightened terms of such treaties as remain to deal with flows to tax havens; more states joining their numbers (thus making being a tax haven itself more competitive); larger states adopting zones or individual tax laws in direct competition with havens; the major states adopting outreach provisions to tackle by other means the loss of tax due to jurisdictional limits (beyond which the havens have to operate); increased enforcement of taxes against taxpayers likely to be using haven routes, both nationally and through international cooperation; less marginal advantage due to a general reduction in direct tax rates; inability to assist as efficiently in reducing other forms of taxation, such as social security taxes and value added tax; and finally, and most recently, closer attention to the extent to which their activities are cloaks for criminal activities rather than mere tax avoidance.

728. Looking ahead, it is perhaps the competition rather than anything else that is likely to bring tax havens within a tolerable level of activity. Their chief attraction is for their handling of savings and inherited wealth. As far as the former is concerned, the logic of free movement of capital and growing globalisation of banking and financial services is already driving down both the taxes on capital income, such as tax on unit trusts (mutual funds) and those on savings transactions of moveable assets, such as stock exchange transfer taxes. There is nothing in current developments to suggest that this trend will reverse, and much to say that it will continue. Behind this are the arguments of economists that the world is not saving enough, and that therefore measures to encourage useful savings will be needed in many economies.

729. Wittingly or otherwise, income taxes are slowly being converted into expenditure taxes, and at the same time are being at the margin superseded by expenditure taxes. Tax havens will have problems legally sheltering taxpayers from expenditure taxes if the expenditure occurs directly or

indirectly within another state's jurisdiction. And if it does not, why should that other state be concerned?

General future trends

730. Aside from tax havens, we must now summarise our thoughts and observations, and raise some outstanding points. We will deal first with the direct taxes.

The base-rate tradeoff

731. We have argued above both from observation and our attempt at modelling, that the trend to wider bases and lower rates of corporate and individual income taxes is not readily reversible.
It is true that widening the bases has proved harder than reducing the rates, but the slack has been taken by transferring the burden to other forms of taxation with some success, by isolating out social welfare costs from the general budget and making it finance itself from its own separate taxes, and – rather less successfully – cutting state budgets. Nonetheless, erosion of the widened bases has already started in some places. It is likely that taxes will therefore ease up, but a corporate rate band of 35% to 40%, with effective reduction of this through an imputation system, is likely to be the most plausible level – or at least the most plausible maximum level – of corporate taxation for some time, with personal income taxes rising to about 50%. If there is to be further reform, the arguments would suggest they will be in the direction of a further reduction in the main rates of direct tax, especially corporate direct taxes, at whatever cost that imposes on the overall fiscal systems by way of losses of reliefs or the increase of other forms of tax.

Double taxation increasingly inevitable

732. There seems no likelihood within any planning horizon of states adopting rules within their national tax systems that will avoid all double taxation. On the contrary, several current trends point the opposite way. First, we have seen the transfer of the link between corporations and states on to the double basis of nationality and residence. Second we have seen the adoption of outreach laws, particularly controlled foreign company legislation. Third, we have seen more rigorous legislation and enforcement at the frontiers and on cross-frontier transactions, through exit charges, transfer pricing and so on. Double taxation relief therefore has an assured future as do double taxation agreements.

Growing numbers of DTAs

733. The logic of the present situation is also that the current momentum behind the growing web of double taxation agreements will make it hard to resist their application to states seeking to add them to their treaty arrangements, and will make it hard to make any significant changes in the general patterns of agreement already established.

Growing disparities between DTAs

734. However, there is likely to be a growing disparity of individual terms within agreements as individual states and regional groupings adopt their own model treaties (witness those of the UN, the USA, the Netherlands, the Andean Pact, ASEAN and Canada), which somewhat contradicts the main argument of this report, that inter state competition will cause the convergence of rates and forms of direct taxes.

When will it end?

735. The key question is, at what point will the web of increasingly varied double tax agreements between an increasing number of countries dealing with increased overlaps but decreasingly different direct taxes of decreasing relative importance to states, collapse?

736. We noted earlier that the logic of present trends is towards a web of many thousands of agreements, being updated at an increased rate, and being subject both to treaty overrides by national legislation and disparate judicial and administrative interpretations and applications. Simply keeping abreast if the system will become increasingly difficult and specialist – and therefore expensive.

737. Yet attempts to break though this web and find multilateral agreement have had extremely limited success. This highlights what has in the past been the success of DTAs, but may in the future prove their weaknesses. They allow states to agree to disagree. Under a double treaty regime no state has to be seen conceding such important principles as the exact way it defines an individual as resident, or its treatment of the consideration for a lease of movable property, or – perhaps with more justice – the limits it imposes on its own tax gatherers in gathering information.

738. This has worked well in the past for sovereign states in the direct tax field, just as it has with the pattern of Bermuda agreement for civil aircraft flights, extradition treaties between pairs of states and other areas where practice has eschewed the multilateral agreement. But just as this is proving increasingly awkward in extradition, and increasingly inconvenient

for those flying – and flying in – civil aircraft, so the strains will show for tax authorities.

A piecemeal multilateral approach?

739. One way forward would be to isolate the different aspects of double tax agreements. This is the approach used elsewhere in international legal diplomacy. For example, states might agree to a multilateral treaty along the lines of article 24 of the OECD Model, the non-discrimination provision. Another area where it might be relatively easy to start would be article 6, and the taxation of land. Another, more controversial example, would be an agreement on the definition of residence of individuals or on permanent establishments, and on tie-breaker rules for residence on a multilateral basis. Even if, in this way, some part of the content of double taxation agreements could be standardised, or the inter-governmental parts of the agreements could be severed from those directly affecting taxpayers, there would a more discipline about the growing tangle of agreements. By being much less ambitious than was the OECD/CE draft, and at the same time recognising (as that draft failed to do) the importance of building in checks and precautions, will progress be easier to make.

Three-state agreements?

740. Another question so far unanswered is the third state problem in double tax agreements. The essential limits to double tax agreements (the residents of the two states, and no inclusion of third parties), whilst realistic in terms of securing past agreement for the reasons just noted, leave the network flawed in other ways, forcing patterns of business on companies that they might not otherwise want, as, for example, the creation of otherwise unneeded subsidiaries. Such problems can be tackled, if ever they are, only through more general agreement. At present there seems little sign of such agreement.

741. In particular, we noted earlier in the text the anomalies caused by the third state problem both in the distortion of treaties by the planner, and the reverse effect. Typically, the response to treaty shopping has caused treaties to include clauses identifying beneficial ownership with the state parties, not third states, thus leaving subsidiaries with third state ownership outside a treaty, even though the parent would be within it, as would an independent company in the state of the subsidiary. This is a particular example of the problem caused by attempting to solve a problem involving several states through a bilateral network. Put simply, it fails to deal with multinational corporate groups.

Growing importance of withholdings

742. Within the provisions of direct relevance to taxpayers (articles 6 to 22), we have seen that the lowering of underlying rates of tax has not yet been accompanied by a general reduction in the withholding taxes. We have argued that withholdings on interest are likely to diminish fast, and have noted the European Commission proposal to do away with withholding on both interest and royalties within the Community. But we have equally noted recent agreement which have maintained, or even increased, withholdings. A maintenance of withholdings amounts to a shift to source based taxing, as the relative withholdings are more important than they were.

Few changes between residence and source competences

743. Elsewhere in those provisions, few changes seem to be emerging, as patterns of income tax and corporate taxes are spread to deal with gaps (as with the absence of capital gains tax in Belgium being covered in the Belgium-Sweden agreement) but with little new happening. This suggests the patterns of those articles will merely develop more complexity and comprehensiveness. At the same time, they are likely increasingly to reflect the aggressive treatment of frontier limits of major states – especially the USA – and contain anti-treaty abuse provisions. This is likely to give rise to an increasing number of disputes in the applications of treaties, especially, and perhaps less obviously, taxpayers will find the application of treaties themselves increasingly producing double taxation and/or serious international compliance costs.

Arbitration?

744. How will these disputes be solved ? There is little movement also on the problem of treaty disputes. The procedures of mutual agreement of the competent authorities and the absence of a binding procedure to deal with disputes on meaning or application (as with article 9) have long been the subject of adverse comments by representatives of taxpayers, but little notice has been taken of this. There have been two cautious steps forward. One is the precedent in the USA-Germany double taxation agreement for an arbitration system on a bilateral basis. The other is the European Community's draft transfer pricing arbitration agreement, although this is a cautious and narrow provision.

745. It may be that, if the European Community finds the newly adopted directive on adjustments of tax in both states after a conflict in transfer pricing ruling to be a success, this will precipitate such a development on a wider basis. Whilst it took 21 years for the draft to be approved, it is a

signal step that a multilateral compulsory procedure is at last starting to be put into place. Reliance on national courts is not enough, but again – aside from this one measure – there is little to suggest that things have yet developed to the stage where such a procedure has become desirable to states. Perhaps the growing web of double taxation agreements will make this so, especially if a lead is given within the Community.

Social security taxes

746. The other major limit on double taxation agreements is the limited number of taxes they cover. Turning to the social security taxes, these are covered by different kinds of agreement, though these are also growing in number. The world-wide attitude that social security taxes are not, somehow, 'taxes' has protected them until recently in most countries from the kind of tax planning so aggressively adopted in common law states (though not civil law or Asian states) for the direct taxes. The pressure, from amongst other sources, of increased costs of such funds throughout the developed world, combined together with the more aggressive advice being accepted by would-be contributors about avoidance possibilities, means that these attitudes will continue spilling out into these forms of tax. Accordingly, they will also become more sophisticated and avoidance-proofed, and presumably therefore the pressure will go on to international issues as well.

VAT

747. There are no double taxation agreements on indirect taxes or VAT. At present, they are largely not needed for VAT, as the number of state now not having a VAT on the destination basis (exempting exports) is diminishing yearly. If, as quite a number of well-placed United States experts are predicting (it might be added, yet again), the USA adopts a VAT, the pattern will truly be all-embracing. That tax will then go through the same rate cutting and base widening exercise that has already started to occur, especially if, as also now seems possible, the USA adopts a very widely based VAT. For example, if they charge VAT on some part of financial services consideration, this will be a more attractive option elsewhere.

Shifts from direct taxes to VAT

748. The shift from direct taxes to VAT will not be reversed.
Unlike the specific excises, VAT is inflation-proof and can collect large amounts of money at seemingly low rates. It purports to be a very visible tax, but psychologically seems not to be. Not least for that reason, it has

distinct attractions to the politician, as well as to the administrator and economist. For similar reasons, VAT is likely to continue to replace more specific taxes on goods and services.

VAT as an origin-based tax?

749. However, it remains to be seen whether the tax stays as a destination-based tax, and is not changed to an origin basis. If the European Commission succeeds in persuading others to its plan, then either many other states will also have to change, or there will be severe mismatching of VAT systems with imports and exports. The kind of clearing house considered as an internal adjustment measure for the Community will not work with third states.

Will double VAT agreements be needed?

750. It may be, therefore that at that point a whole series of bilateral agreements or adjustments will be needed. But will a third state agree individually with each of the twelve Member States, or will there be a multilateral agreement? Certainly, aspects of the multilateral regime applying to customs duties could be borrowed. But it may be that the Commission, having so far not come up with any positive answers to these problems, or clear answers about adjustments in the Community, fails to persuade all Member States as to the wisdom of its ideas. Our models suggested that the import neutrality of the present form of VAT proved expensive to exporters unless they are also importers, but there are balancing factors at work which may make the existing scheme seem the better arrangement. If it does, what form will these agreements take? How will they deal with the situation where the export state is a destination-based VAT state, whilst the import state is an origin-based VAT state? That is a problem largely not encountered with direct taxes.

Customs duties and other minor taxes will decline

751. Finally, behind all these moves, the old, tried taxes will fade away. Customs duties will be one victim. Given the very considerable degree of coordination of the technical side of customs duties, combined with the positive achievements of GATT, there will be a loss of expertise in resolving inter-state tax disputes unless these lessons can be transferred to the handling of other taxes. Other taxes such as stamp duties also seem to be going out of fashion. It is part, we suspect, of the increasing convergence which will make the imposition of major new taxes
very difficult. However the attractions of increasing local taxes, and also fees and charges, which do not seem to have an international element, will be considerable.

752. If the above is so, then the next few years are going to see growing aggression and growing complexity in enforcing the direct taxes internationally at a time when both should be easing. There will be a growing complexity particularly in the network of double tax agreements. Pressures will build up to provide multilateral answers, growing inter-state assistance and some form of neutral dispute system. Failing that, the sustained pressure on national tax authorities from increasingly well advised and well informed – and increasingly mobile and international – taxpayers will make their life steadily harder and their laws steadily more intricate.

753. Equally, pressures will affect the balance between the direct taxes and other taxes, making VAT in particular an attractive solution. This will enable states to decrease their direct tax rates in all areas but particularly on savings, and will leave them with a permanent pressure to increase bases rather than rates. The solution also lies with social security taxes (though that will start hitting some of the same problems as the direct taxes) and local taxes and charges. All these will cumulatively shift the balance in international taxation away from states of residence to source states – that is, if residence continues to be a relevant basis except in name, and is not replaced by nationality of the taxpayer, or the recognition, in a developed state, that the ability, under the immigration laws, to be present, is a valuable commodity for which tax is part of the price.

754. National tax reforms started from a desire to make life simpler. They have failed, and will continue to fail, in that aim.
At the same time they fed a process of tax competition, which has acquired a momentum of its own. The result is a situation where states are forced towards the dilemma of both competing with each other and yet cooperating with each other to increasing degrees.
International tax is therefore assured an active future.

Bibliography

The folllowing works have been referred to in the text or in its preparation. I have added some personal comments about the more important of the sources as a brief guide to readers who do not know them. Some references are made to individual articles in periodicals. Where the periodicals contain a number of relevant articles, this is noted and no attempt has been made to list each article separately.

It must also be added that increasingly the data on which essays such as this draw is available in machine-readable form. Current versions of all double tax agreements are available on CD-Rom from the International Bureau of Fiscal Documentation, as are several other specific and relevant databases, eg those on corporate taxation and on private investment income in Organisation for Economic Cooperation and Development states. OECD statistics are available in machine readable form, and a number of newspapers and journals are also held on database. English language texts, including tax notes, treaties, and an increasing number of journals, plus the Tax Notes and Tax Notes International services are available on the LEXIS database. European Community texts are available on a number of databases such as CERES and JUSTIS. A number of these sources were used in preparing this essay. Their influence must increase, and as it does, the need for indexes and secondary access to sources will decline. That itself is an influence which this essay stresses, and to that extent bibliographies such as this are of declining value.

With the caveats noted above, the reader's attention is drawn to the following sources, the emphasis being mainly on the literature of the last ten years:

1. Other bibliographies:

Owens E and Hovemeyer G, *Bibliography on Taxation of Foreign Operations and Foreigners,* (Harvard Law School International Tax Program, 1976 and 1983).

Soos PE, *Selected Bibliography on Income Tax Administration in Developed and Developing Countries,* International Bureau for Fiscal Documentation and Harvard, 1989.

2. Selected sources:

Aaron HJ and Galper H, *Assessing Tax Reform,* (Brookings Institution, Washington, 1985).

African Tax Systems, looseleaf, updated (International Bureau for Fiscal Documentation, Amsterdam).

Asian-Pacific Tax Conference, *Current Issues and Trends in Taxation and Investment,* (Asian-Pacific Tax and Investment Research Centre, Singapore, 1989). Papers from the Centre's fifth conference.

Baker, P, *Double Taxation Agreements and International Tax Law,* (Sweet & Maxwell, London, 1991). Contains a thorough survey of the jurisprudence and literature of major states in using the OECD model double taxation convention in practice.

Becker H and Wurm FJ (eds), *Treaty Shopping: an Emerging Tax Issue and Its Present Status in Various Countries,* (Kluwer, Netherlands, 1988).

Bird RM and Oldman O, *Taxation in Developing Countries,* (John Hopkins University Press, Baltimore, 1990). A new fourth edition, after an interval, of this seminal book of readings.

Bischell J, *International Tax Planning after the Tax Reform Act 1986, (Matthew Bender, New York, 1989).*

Block W and Walker M (eds), *Taxation: An international perspective,* (The Fraser Institute, Vancouver, Canada, 1984). Papers from an international symposium held in 1980, highlighting some of the problems which subsequent reforms have started to address.

Bradford DF, *Untangling the Income Tax* , (Harvard University Press, Cambridge, United States of America, 1986).

Brean D, *International issues in Taxation: The Canadian Perspective,* (Canadian Tax Foundation, Toronto, 1984).

Brennan G and Buchanan JM, *The Power to Tax,* (Cambridge University Press, United States of America, 1980).

Bulletin for International Fiscal Documentation, monthly journal including the official journal of the International Fiscal Association (International Bureau of Fiscal Documentation, Amsterdam). Many relevant articles drawn worldwide.

Business International Corporation, *Meeting the Challenge of Global Tax Reform, (BIC, New York, 1989).*

Canadian Government, Goods and Services Tax: An Overview, (Government Printer, Ottawa, 1990).

Canadian Tax Journal, periodical publication of the influential Canadian Tax Foundation, Toronto, also accompanied by occasional Canadian Tax Papers, and the publication of annual conference proceedings. Contain and include many valuable discussions on current developments.

Chown JF, *Company Tax Harmonisation in the European Community,* (Institute of Directors, London, 1989).

Cnossen S (ed), *Tax Coordination in the European Community,* (Kluwer, Netherlands, 1987). A most valuable series of essays by leading commentators on past and possible developments in Community taxation .

Commission on Taxation (Ireland), *First Report, (1982), Second Report, (1982), Third Report, (1984), (Stationery Office, Dublin).*

Confédération Fiscale Européenne, *Taxpayer Protection, (International Bureau of Fiscal Documentation, Amsterdam, 1990).* Comparative summaries of the current (1989) position in ten major states of Europe.

Coopers & Lybrand, Deloittes, International Tax Summaries, (Coopers & Lybrand, Deloittes, annual). Useful brief summaries of tax systems of many states.

Diamond WH and Diamond DB, International Tax Treaties of All Nations, (Matthew Bender, New York, 1985). Looseleaf, updated, a standard work of reference, but being superseded by data bases.

Diamond WH and Diamond DB, *Tax Havens of the World,* (Matthew Bender, New York, 1985).

Doernberg, RL, International Taxation, *West Publishing Co, ST Pauls, Minn, United States of America, 1989).* A summary of the United States provisions on foreign taxation.

Economic Perspectives, periodical. The Summer 1987 number includes an important symposium on tax reform.

Edwardes-Ker, M, *International Tax Treaty Service,* (In-Depth Publishing Co, looseleaf service last updated 1990). Perhaps the most thorough survey of national practice in the use of double taxation agreements.

European Communities, Commission, *Completing the Internal Market,* (Brussels, June 1985). The Commission White Paper with which the campaign for the Single European market was successfully launched.

European Communities, Commission, *Completion of the Internal Market: Approximation of Indirect Tax Rates and Harmonisation of Indirect Tax Structure,* (Brussels, 1987 COM(87) 320). This was the 'global communication' released by the European Community Commission in 1987 together with COM (87) 321 through 328, which provided the supporting details and proposals, to spell out what the Commission then saw to be the necessary tax changes to achieve the Single European market. The proposals were replaced by others through 1990 and 1991.

European Taxation, monthly journal including the official journal of the Confederation Fiscale Europeenne (International Bureau of Fiscal Documentation, Amsterdam). Numerous excellent relevant articles and documents, supported fully by a *Supplementary Service* including full English texts of many documents (also available as a database).

Fiscal Studies, bimonthly (Basil Blackwell, Oxford). Journal of the United Kingdom's influential Institute for Fiscal Studies.

Gillis M (ed), *Tax Reform in Developing Countries,* (Duke University Press, North Carolina, United States of America, 1989).

Grundy M, *Tax havens: A World Survey,* (Sweet & Maxwell, London, several editions). Brief vignettes of selected low tax countries.

International Bar Association, *Tax Avoidance, Tax Evasion,* (Sweet & Maxwell, London, several editions). Comparative summaries from several major states.

International Bureau of Fiscal Documentation, *European Tax Handbook,* annual summaries of all taxes and contributions.

International Bureau of Fiscal Documentation, *Guides to European Taxation,* six sets of volumes, looseleaf, updated (International Bureau for Fiscal Documentation, Amsterdam). Comprehensively covers all aspects of European and European Community taxation.

International Monetary Fund, *Government Finance Statistics Yearbook,* (annual).

International VAT Monitor, monthly journal (International Bureau of Fiscal Documentation, Amsterdam.)

Intertax, monthly journal, Kluwer, Netherlands. Has expanded over recent years to become a major journal in the field, with several valuable special numbers.

Kay JM and King M, *The British Tax System,* (several editions, Oxford University Press). The leading United Kingdom general survey of taxes, tax policies and tax reforms.

Kingson C, *"The Coherence of International Taxation",* (1981) 81 Columbia Law Review 1151. A wide ranging, major analysis of United States of America international tax system design problems.

Langer, MJ, *Practical International Tax Planning,* (Practising Law Institute, New York, several editions).

Lee C, Pearson M and Smith SR, *Fiscal Harmonisation: An Analysis of the European Commission's Proposals,* (Institute for Fiscal Studies Report Series No 28, Institute for Fiscal Studies, 1988). A critique of the 1987 European Community proposals exposing a number of weaknesses in analysis of the European Community approach.

McDaniel P and Surrey SS (eds), *International Aspects of Tax Expenditures: A Comparative Survey,* (Kluwer, Netherlands, 1984).

McLure CE Jr, *The Value-Added Tax: Key to Deficit Reduction,* (American Enterprise Institute, Washington, 1987). An argument still to be realised?

Martha RSJ, *The jurisdiction to tax in International Law: Theory and Practice of Legislative Fiscal Jurisdiction,* (Kluwer, Netherlands, 1989). Despite limitations and an a priori approach, this is the best study so far on often-ignored jurisdictional issues.

Meade Report, *The Structure and Reform of Direct Taxation,* (Allen and Unwin, London, for the Institute for Fiscal Studies, 1978). As near as the United Kingdom came to having a government commission during this period examining desirable patterns of tax reform, this report argued for a personal expenditure tax and cash-flow corporation taxation.

Mintz J and Whalley J (eds), *The Economic Impacts of Tax Reform,* (Canadian Tax Foundation, Toronto, 1989).

Musgrave RA, *Fiscal Systems,* (Yale University Press, 1969). A powerful and in part prophetic volume.

Musgrave RA, Musgrave PB and Bird RM, *Public Finance in Theory and Practice,* (several editions, McGraw-Hill). A wide-ranging primer by acknowledged grand masters (and grand mistress) of the field.

Newbery D and Stern N (eds), *The Theory of Taxation for Developing Countries,* (Oxford University Press, Oxford, 1987). A powerful series of essays by economists advancing theories for tax structures in developing states, supported by case studies.

Organisation for Econimc Cooperation and Development, *Economies in Transition,* (1989). Chapter 5 reviews the scale of the problems facing the newly realigned economies of central and eastern Europe.

Organisation for Economic Cooperation and Development, Issues in International Taxation Series:
1 *International Tax Avoidance and Evasion,* four studies, (1987)
2 *Thin capitalisation. Taxation of Entertainers, Artistes and Sportsmen,* (1987)
3 *Consequences of Foreign Exchange Gains and Losses,* (1988).

Organisation for Economic Cooperation and Development, *Personal Income Tax Systems under Changing Economic Conditions,* (1986).

Organisation for Economic Cooperation and Development, *Revenue Statistics of OECD member Countries,* (annual). Detailed analyses of revenue receipts of all kinds annually since 1965. An invaluable source of comparisons.

Organisation for Economic Cooperation and Development, *Taxation in Developed Countries,* (1988). A symposium organised by the French Government in cooperation with the OECD in 1987 producing a valuable range of papers and views.

Organisation for Economic Cooperation and Development, *The Taxation of Fringe Benefits,* (1988).

Organisation for Economic Cooperation and Development, *Taxation of Net Wealth, Capital Transfers and Capital Gains of Individuals,* (1988)

Organisation for Economic Cooperation and Development, *Taxing Consumption,* (1988). A thorough and valuable study of the evolution of Value added tax and its use by OECD member states.

Organisation for Economic Co-operation and Development, *Trends in International Taxation,* (1985). A report of the OECD Fiscal Affairs Committee predating the major recent changes.

Pechman JA (ed), *What should be taxed: Income or Expenditure?,* (Brookings Institution, Washington, 1980).

Pechman JA (ed), *Comparative Tax Systems: Europe, Canada and Japan,* (Tax Analysts, Arlington, United States of America, 1987).

Pechman JA (ed), *World Tax Reform: A Progress Report,* (Brookings Institution, Washington, 1988). Papers and comments from a 1987 conference with an impressive range of expertise present looking at the aftermath of the 1986 reforms.

Phillips, JS, *Tax Treaty Networks,* (1991, expanded from 1989, Worldwide Information, London). A comparative survey of the terms of the mutual tax treaties of the 12 leading economies, with commentary.

Pires M, *International Juridical Double Taxation of income,* (Kluwer, Netherlands, 1989).

Price Waterhouse, *Corporate Taxes – A worldwide Summary,* (Price Waterhouse, London and New York, annual). A comprehensive, concise and regularly updated summary of key relevant features of most states' business taxes. Most useful for a brief introduction and comparison.

Price Waterhouse, *Individual Taxes – A Worldwide Guide,* (Price Waterhouse, annual). Companion volume to the corporate taxes guide above.

Rose R and Karran T, *Taxation by Political Inertia,* (George Allen & Unwin, London, 1987)

Rosenblaum HT and Langbin SL, *"United States Tax Treaty Policy – An Overall View",* (1981) 19 Columbia Journal of Transnational Law 359.

Ross SG, *"A perspective on international tax policy",* Tax Notes, 1985, 701.

Sandford C and Robinson A, *Tax policy-making in the United Kingdom,* (1983).

Spitz B, *Tax Havens Encyclopedia,* (Butterworths, London, looseleaf).

Stein H (ed), *Tax policy in the Twenty-First Century,* (John Wiley & Sons, New York, 1988). Papers from a wide-ranging seminar held in Washington DC in 1987).

Tait AA, *Value Added Tax: International Practice and Problems,* (International Monetary Fund, Washington, 1988). Although not an official International Monetary Fund work, this is an excellent and important survey of the evolution of value added tax.

Tax News Service, fortnightly, (International Bureau for Fiscal Documentation, Amsterdam). Brief summaries of changes both to national tax laws and to tax treaties.

Terra B, *Sales Taxation: the Case of Value Added Tax in the European Community,* (Kluwer, Netherlands, 1988).

United Kingdom Government, *Green Paper on Corporation Tax,* (London, HMSO, 1982, Cmnd. 8456).

United Nations, *Manual for the Negotiation of Bilateral Tax Treaties betwee[n] Developed and Developing Countries,* (United Nations, New York, 1979, U[N] Doc ST/ESA/94).

United Nations Center on Transnational Corporations, *International Income Taxation and Developing Countries,* (United Nations, New York, 1988).

United States of America Treasury, *Blueprints for Basic Tax Reform,* (United States of America Government Printer, Washington, 1977). At the official level, perhaps this is where the current wave of reforms really started.

United States of America Treasury, *Tax Reform for Fairness, Simplicity and Economic Growth,* (United States of America Government Printer, Washington, 1984). A good example of how to make an official publication a hostage to fortune by its title alone! The follow through was the Tax Reform Act 1986.

Van Raad, K, *Model Income Tax Treaties,* (Kluwer, Deventer, Netherlands, 1983). Contains the texts of the OECD, United Nations and also United States of America Treasury Model double taxation conventions in useful comparative form. For a comment by the same author on the Netherlands model, see (1988) Intertax 241.

Van Raad, K, *Nondiscrimination in International Tax Law,* (Kluwer, Netherlands, 1986).

Webber C and Wildavsky A, *A History of Taxation and Expenditure in the Western World,* (New York, Simon and Schuster, 1986). Sounds overambitious, but goes a long way to meeting the challenge of its title.

World Bank, *World Development Reports,* (annual, World Bank, Washington). The 1988 Report is particularly interesting in connection with tax reform.

Mintz J and Whalley J (eds), *The Economic Impacts of Tax Reform,* (Canadian Tax Foundation, Toronto, 1989).

Musgrave RA, *Fiscal Systems,* (Yale University Press, 1969). A powerful and in part prophetic volume.

Musgrave RA, Musgrave PB and Bird RM, *Public Finance in Theory and Practice,* (several editions, McGraw-Hill). A wide-ranging primer by acknowledged grand masters (and grand mistress) of the field.

Newbery D and Stern N (eds), *The Theory of Taxation for Developing Countries,* (Oxford University Press, Oxford, 1987). A powerful series of essays by economists advancing theories for tax structures in developing states, supported by case studies.

Organisation for Econimc Cooperation and Development, *Economies in Transition,* (1989). Chapter 5 reviews the scale of the problems facing the newly realigned economies of central and eastern Europe.

Organisation for Economic Cooperation and Development, Issues in International Taxation Series:
1 *International Tax Avoidance and Evasion,* four studies, (1987)
2 *Thin capitalisation. Taxation of Entertainers, Artistes and Sportsmen,* (1987)
3 *Consequences of Foreign Exchange Gains and Losses,* (1988).

Organisation for Economic Cooperation and Development, *Personal Income Tax Systems under Changing Economic Conditions,* (1986).

Organisation for Economic Cooperation and Development, *Revenue Statistics of OECD member Countries,* (annual). Detailed analyses of revenue receipts of all kinds annually since 1965. An invaluable source of comparisons.

Organisation for Economic Cooperation and Development, *Taxation in Developed Countries,* (1988). A symposium organised by the French Government in cooperation with the OECD in 1987 producing a valuable range of papers and views.

Organisation for Economic Cooperation and Development, *The Taxation of Fringe Benefits,* (1988).

Organisation for Economic Cooperation and Development, *Taxation of Net Wealth, Capital Transfers and Capital Gains of Individuals,* (1988)

Organisation for Economic Cooperation and Development, *Taxing Consumption,* (1988). A thorough and valuable study of the evolution of Value added tax and its use by OECD member states.

Organisation for Economic Co-operation and Development, *Trends in International Taxation,* (1985). A report of the OECD Fiscal Affairs Committee predating the major recent changes.

Pechman JA (ed), *What should be taxed: Income or Expenditure?,* (Brookings Institution, Washington, 1980).

Pechman JA (ed), *Comparative Tax Systems: Europe, Canada and Japan,* (Tax Analysts, Arlington, United States of America, 1987).

Pechman JA (ed), *World Tax Reform: A Progress Report,* (Brookings Institution, Washington, 1988). Papers and comments from a 1987 conference with an impressive range of expertise present looking at the aftermath of the 1986 reforms.

Phillips, JS, *Tax Treaty Networks,* (1991, expanded from 1989, Worldwide Information, London). A comparative survey of the terms of the mutual tax treaties of the 12 leading economies, with commentary.

Pires M, *International Juridical Double Taxation of income,* (Kluwer, Netherlands, 1989).

Price Waterhouse, *Corporate Taxes – A worldwide Summary,* (Price Waterhouse, London and New York, annual). A comprehensive, concise and regularly updated summary of key relevant features of most states' business taxes. Most useful for a brief introduction and comparison.

Price Waterhouse, *Individual Taxes – A Worldwide Guide,* (Price Waterhouse, annual). Companion volume to the corporate taxes guide above.

Rose R and Karran T, *Taxation by Political Inertia,* (George Allen & Unwin, London, 1987)

Rosenblaum HT and Langbin SL, *"United States Tax Treaty Policy – An Overall View",* (1981) 19 Columbia Journal of Transnational Law 359.

Ross SG, *"A perspective on international tax policy",* Tax Notes, 1985, 701.

Sandford C and Robinson A, *Tax policy-making in the United Kingdom,* (1983).

Spitz B, *Tax Havens Encyclopedia,* (Butterworths, London, looseleaf).

Stein H (ed), *Tax policy in the Twenty-First Century,* (John Wiley & Sons, New York, 1988). Papers from a wide-ranging seminar held in Washington DC in 1987).

Tait AA, *Value Added Tax: International Practice and Problems,* (International Monetary Fund, Washington, 1988). Although not an official International Monetary Fund work, this is an excellent and important survey of the evolution of value added tax.

Tax News Service, fortnightly, (International Bureau for Fiscal Documentation, Amsterdam). Brief summaries of changes both to national tax laws and to tax treaties.

Terra B, *Sales Taxation: the Case of Value Added Tax in the European Community,* (Kluwer, Netherlands, 1988).

United Kingdom Government, *Green Paper on Corporation Tax,* (London, HMSO, 1982, Cmnd. 8456).

United Nations, *Manual for the Negotiation of Bilateral Tax Treaties between Developed and Developing Countries,* (United Nations, New York, 1979, UN Doc ST/ESA/94).

United Nations Center on Transnational Corporations, *International Income Taxation and Developing Countries,* (United Nations, New York, 1988).

United States of America Treasury, *Blueprints for Basic Tax Reform,* (United States of America Government Printer, Washington, 1977). At the official level, perhaps this is where the current wave of reforms really started.

United States of America Treasury, *Tax Reform for Fairness, Simplicity and Economic Growth,* (United States of America Government Printer, Washington, 1984). A good example of how to make an official publication a hostage to fortune by its title alone! The follow through was the Tax Reform Act 1986.

Van Raad, K, *Model Income Tax Treaties,* (Kluwer, Deventer, Netherlands, 1983). Contains the texts of the OECD, United Nations and also United States of America Treasury Model double taxation conventions in useful comparative form. For a comment by the same author on the Netherlands model, see (1988) Intertax 241.

Van Raad, K, *Nondiscrimination in International Tax Law,* (Kluwer, Netherlands, 1986).

Webber C and Wildavsky A, *A History of Taxation and Expenditure in the Western World,* (New York, Simon and Schuster, 1986). Sounds overambitious, but goes a long way to meeting the challenge of its title.

World Bank, *World Development Reports,* (annual, World Bank, Washington). The 1988 Report is particularly interesting in connection with tax reform.